Ribbon Embroidery BY MACHINE

OTHER BOOKS AVAILABLE FROM CHILTON

Contemporary Quilting

All Quilt Blocks Are Not Square, by Debra Wagner

Barbara Johannah's Crystal Piecing

The Complete Book of Machine Quilting, Second Edition, by Robbie and Tony Fanning

Contemporary Quilting Techniques, by Pat Cairns

Creative Triangles for Quilters, by Janet B. Elwin

Dye It! Paint It! Quilt It!, by Joyce Mori and Cynthia Myerberg

Fast Patch, by Anita Hallock

Precision Pieced Quilts Using the Foundation Method, by Jane Hall and Dixie Haywood

The Quilter's Guide to Rotary Cutting, by Donna Poster

Scrap Quilts Using Fast Patch, by Anita Hallock

Stars Galore and Even More, by Donna Poster

Stitch 'n' Quilt, by Kathleen Eaton

Super Simple Quilts, by Kathleen Eaton

Three-Dimensional Pieced Quilts, by Jodie Davis

Craft Kaleidoscope

The Banner Book, Ruth Ann Lowery

The Crafter's Guide to Glues, by Tammy Young

Creating and Crafting Dolls, by Eloise Piper and Mary Dilligan

Fabric Crafts and Other Fun with Kids, by Susan Parker Beck and Charlou Lunsford

Quick and Easy Ways with Ribbon, by Ceci Johnson

Learn Bearmaking, by Judi Maddigan

Stamping Made Easy, by Nancy Ward

Creative Machine Arts

Machine Embroidery, by Susan Rock

ABCs of Serging, by Tammy Young and Lori Bottom

Affordable Heirlooms, by Edna Powers and Gaye Kriegel

Alphabet Stitchery by Hand & Machine, by Carolyn Vosburg Hall

The Button Lover's Book, by Marilyn Green

Claire Shaeffer's Fabric Sewing Guide

The Complete Book of Machine Embroidery, by Robbie and Tony Fanning

Craft an Elegant Wedding, by Tammy Young and Naomi Baker

Distinctive Serger Gifts and Crafts, by Naomi Baker and Tammy Young

Gail Brown's All-New Instant Interiors

Hold It! How to Sew Bags, Totes, Duffels, Pouches, and More, by Nancy Restuccia

How to Make Soft Jewelry, by Jackie Dodson

Innovative Serging, by Gail Brown and Tammy Young

The New Creative Serging Illustrated, by Pati Palmer, Gail Brown, and Sue Green

Quick Napkin Creations, by Gail Brown

Second Stitches: Recycle as You Sew, by Susan Parker

Serge a Simple Project, by Tammy Young and Naomi Baker

Serge Something Super for Your Kids, by Cindy Cummins

Sew Any Patch Pocket, by Claire Shaeffer

Sew Any Set-In Pocket, by Claire Shaeffer

Sew Sensational Gifts, by Naomi Baker and Tammy Young

Sewing and Collecting Vintage Fashions, by Eileen MacIntosh

Shirley Botsford's Daddy's Ties

Soft Gardens: Make Flowers with Your Sewing Machine, by Yvonne Perez-Collins

The Stretch & Sew Guide to Sewing Knits, by Ann Person

Twenty Easy Machine-Made Rugs, by Jackie Dodson

The Ultimate Serger Answer Guide, by Naomi Baker, Gail Brown and Cindy Kacynski

Know Your Serger Series, by Tammy Young and Naomi Baker

Know Your baby lock

Sew & Serge Series, by Jackie Dodson and Jan Saunders

Sew & Serge Pillows! Pillows! Pillows!

Sew & Serge Terrific Textures

StarWear

Dazzle, by Linda Fry Kenzle

Embellishments, by Linda Fry Kenzle

Jan Saunders' Wardrobe Quick-Fixes

Make It Your Own, by Lori Bottom and Ronda Chaney

Mary Mulari's Garments with Style

A New Serge in Wearable Art, by Ann Boyce

Pattern-Free Fashions, by Mary Lee Trees Cole

Shirley Adams' Belt Bazaar

Sweatshirts with Style, by Mary Mulari

Teach Yourself to Sew Better, by Jan Saunders

A Step-by-Step Guide to Your New Home

A Step-by-Step Guide to Your Sewing Machine

Ribbon Embroidery BY MACHINE

Marie Duncan and Betty Farrell

Chilton
BOOK COMPANY
Radnor, Pennsylvania

Published in Radnor, Pennsylvania 19089, by Chilton Book Company

COVER DESIGN BY ANTHONY JACOBSON
INTERIOR DESIGN BY STAN GREEN/GREEN GRAPHICS
ILLUSTRATIONS BY MARIE DUNCAN
PHOTOGRAPHY BY DONNA CHIARELLI

Manufactured in the United States of America

Library of Congress Cataloging-in-Publication Data

Duncan, Marie.
Ribbon embroidery by machine / Marie Duncan and Betty Farrell.
p. cm.
Includes index.
ISBN 0-8019-8783-0
1. Silk ribbon embroidery. 2. Embroidery, Machine. 3. Embroidery, Machine—Patterns. I. Farrell, Betty. II. Title.
TT778.S46D86 1996 96-20437
746.44'028—dc20 CIP

1 2 3 4 5 6 7 8 9 0 5 4 3 2 1 0 9 8 7 6

Contents

Chapter 3. Stitches 9

Chapter 4. Flowers 17

Chapter 5. Garden Containers 33

Chapter 9. Projects 57

Preface

Drum roll, please! As computers, faxes, and E-mail are revolutionizing the business world, we're revolutionizing ribbon embroidery with a new technique that we're unveiling in this book. Ribbon embroidery by machine takes a centuries–old technique and adapts it to the sewing machine. Now, the silk ribbons of the past are available in many colors and sizes. And synthetic ribbons and textured threads have expanded the creative possibilities even further.

If you're anything like us, you probably don't need another hobby to envelop you. But our creative hobbies are what keep us going. We've worked together and independently to formulate, plan, compile, and create a book that we hope will enhance and expand your creative territories. And so we invite you to join us and enjoy, enjoy. . .

Read, practice, and create, and then enjoy the compliments and newfound pleasures that come your way.

Acknowledgments

No book is finished without help. We thank our families who were willing to eat take-out meals and enjoy leftovers so we could have a few more minutes to work on this book.

We also thank our friends who loaned us samples and did proofreading when our eyes could see no more. Amy Opalk was a student in one of Marie's classes. She caught the "ribbon-embroidery-by-machine fever." Our thanks to Amy for loaning us her projects, which you see throughout the book.

An up-close look at ribbon-embroidered flowers reveals the simplicity of the stitching. A variety of ribbon colors and blossom types adds to the garden look.

CHAPTER ONE

Introduction and Background

A BRIEF LOOK AT RIBBON EMBROIDERY

Ribbon embroidery is a technique of fabric embellishment that originally was popular in the 1800s, when it often was applied to undergarments and afternoon attire. Most of the silk ribbon embroidery of this time was done with subtle tone-on-tone shading. At first, ribbon embroidery was available only to the wealthy because of the cost of the silk and the need to hire sewers to perform the time-consuming technique. Some of the early ribbon-embroidered garments that are on exhibit in museums show exquisite attention to detail, attesting to the many hours of labor that went into them.

Ribbon embroidery is enjoying a resurgence of popularity, and most of the work being done today still is sewn by hand. Ribbon embroidery by hand is a relaxing, gratifying technique you can call on when your sewing machine isn't available, such as when traveling or commuting. And ribbon embroidery by machine is equally gratifying—flowers and foliage take shape so quickly. It's one of those techniques that keeps you saying "just one more" until, before you know it, it's after midnight and you have to force yourself to stop.

Today, ribbon embroidery appears on everything from delicate lingerie to teddy bears, quilts, and sport clothing. It's such a versatile technique that it looks as beautiful done in tone-on-tone shades as it does with lots of color contrast. The range of available colors runs from subdued to vibrant. You can achieve just about any effect you desire, and the current popularity of wearable art creates lots of possibilities for showing off your ribbon embroidery.

A NEW APPROACH TO RIBBON EMBROIDERY

This book will introduce you to the wonderful new world of ribbon embroidery by machine. Soon, you'll be embellishing clothes, teddy bears, Christmas stockings, picture frames, and so much more. Ribbon embroidery is fast, easy, and fun, but most importantly, you can do it on any sewing machine—from a reliable straight machine to the fanciest computerized model.

Ribbon embroidery by machine is a fascinating craft with unlimited potential. Once you've mastered the basic techniques and stitches, you can develop your own designs and ideas. Whenever we teach a new beginner class, at least one new stitch or flower

always is invented. We've included many of them for you in this book.

We were intrigued by the appearance of traditional hand ribbon embroidery. Being "machine people," we usually didn't have the time or the patience to embroider by hand. And, we were won over by machine embroidery's many benefits: Your embroidery goes much faster, and because it's done on the surface—the ribbon isn't pulled through the fabric—you can embroider heavy, dense, and lightweight fabrics that are difficult to embroider by hand. As we adapted hand stitches to the machine, we also developed a number of techniques that are easier to do by machine than they are by hand.

We hope the ideas in this book will spark your imagination and get you excited about ribbon embroidery. A sewer first looks at everything and then takes in the details and the construction techniques. Now, when you look around, we hope you'll be saying, "I could do that with ribbon embroidery on my sewing machine."

We've organized the book into three basic sections. Preparing for stitching, learning the basic stitches, and combining the stitches into projects. The stitches are the backbone of the book. You'll want to read the section on stitches and try out each one. Then as you delve into the flowers, bugs, and other designs, you'll know how to make the various stitches we suggest. To locate the materials you'll need, try local fabric stores, sewing-machine dealers, and crafts stores. If you have a problem finding everything you need, try the mail-order sources for specific products listed on page 84.

Sit down with book in hand and start sewing. If you run into trouble, check our hints on page 5 for possible remedies. Refer to the instructions for the basic stitches whenever you need to refresh your memory about a particular stitch or technique.

Ideas for ribbon embroidery projects are everywhere. For inspiration, look at seed catalogs, greeting cards, and other embroidery books, whether hand or machine. Look for shapes, color combinations, and general effects that please you. Traditional silk ribbon embroidery books are wonderful references for floral combinations, arrangements, and colors.

We'll introduce you to some basic practice projects, and you can take it from there. Lets get going!

CHAPTER TWO

Getting Ready to Stitch

Assemble basic sewing supplies and equipment. Start with a few of your favorite colors of ribbon, add a few other colors for contrast, and let the fun of ribbon embroidery by machine begin.

SUPPLIES

Sewing Machine

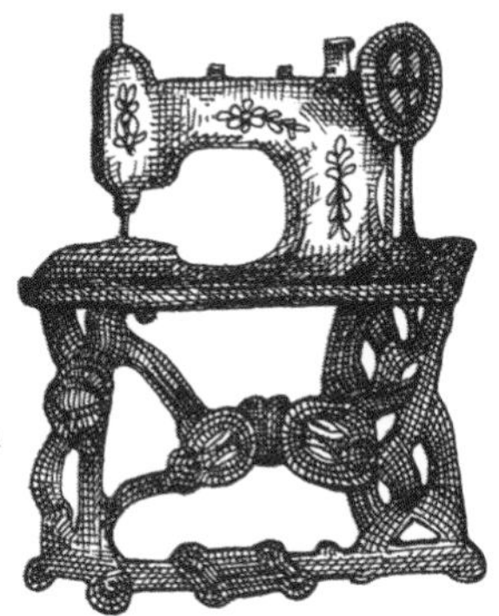

You can use any sewing machine for machine ribbon embroidery because the only stitch you need is the straight stitch. A machine that lets you lower or cover the feed dogs is a definite asset. However, a machine with an electronic needle stop-down setting is a great advantage. The more stitch-by-stitch control you have, the better.

Fabric

You can choose just about any type of background fabric for your stitching. We've worked on both ready-to-wear garments and those we've sewn ourselves, and have found that the secret to success is to match the type of embroidery to the fabric—bolder designs and stitches for heavier fabrics and finer, delicate patterns for lightweight fabrics. Ribbon embroidery is so versatile that you can work it on the finest silk as well as the heaviest denim.

Silk (or rayon silky) ribbon generally can be washed or dry-cleaned. We've hand- and machine-washed our embroidered items with good results. Just be sure to follow the care instructions that accompanied the garment or fabric you embroidered. Test bright-colored silk ribbon for colorfastness by dipping a piece in cool water. Allow the ribbon to soak for a few minutes, then transfer the ribbon to white toweling. Check the color of the water and the white toweling for bleeding. If the color ran, rinse the ribbon until the water is clear to prevent further bleeding. After stitching your project, launder the item only in cold water for the first few washings. Silk ribbon can be machine-dried, and there's no need for pressing.

If you choose to dry-clean an embroidered item, caution the dry cleaner not to press over the worked embroidery, which would flatten it.

Hoop

You'll need a 5" to 6" embroidery hoop. Both wooden and spring hoops work well; just be certain that the hoop will fit under the needle of your sewing machine and will hold the fabric taut. If you're working on delicate fabric such as silk or fine cotton, you may want to wrap the hoop with twill tape to minimize abrasion when you place the fabric in the hoop. Knits don't require any special attention, but be careful not to stretch the fabric as you place it in the hoop. Spring hoops work better for knits. As with any embroidery, remove the fabric from the hoop when you're not stitching to avoid difficult-to-remove hoop marks.

Thread

"Invisible" monofilament thread is used in both the top threading of the machine and in the bobbin. The invisible thread available today is different from that sold 20 years ago. It's soft, pliable, and easy to sew with. A number of manufacturers make monofilament

thread in smoke color as well as clear. We like working with invisible thread because it eliminates changing your machine thread color. When working with very dark ribbons or thread, you may want to use smoke-color thread; clear thread is translucent and virtually disappears. Generally, your ribbon will cover the machine stitches anyway.

You'll also get satisfactory results with polyester and polyester/cotton threads, but you'll need to change the colors of your needle and bobbin threads to match the ribbon colors. Also be aware that polyester and polyester/cotton threads don't tend to be as invisible as monofilament thread.

Ribbon

Embroidery ribbon is different from the decorative ribbon you buy at fabric stores. It's made of 100 percent silk or sometimes a synthetic such as polyester or rayon. Silk embroidery ribbon is extremely soft and pliable, letting you fold and bend it to form beautiful flowers and foliage. Embroidery ribbon comes in 2mm, 4mm, 7mm, and 13mm widths. The 4mm width is the most popular and comes in the greatest number of colors—about 150.

Thanks to the popularity of ribbon embroidery, there are many different brands and types of ribbon available. Some are of better quality than others. Be sure the ribbon you choose is colorfast if you intend to wash or dry-clean the embroidered item.

Needle

Always start each project with a new size 80/12 universal needle in your sewing machine. Be aware that if your needle has a burr or rough spot on it, it will snag the delicate ribbon. If snagging occurs, change the needle immediately.

Markers

Air-soluble markers are available in many colors. Marks made with an air-soluble marker will disappear from your fabric 12 to 24 hours after you apply them. If you use a water-soluble marker, you'll need to spritz the garment with water when you've finished embroidering or launder the garment before wearing it. Use chalk pencils or tailor's chalk on dark colors. Fine-line markers work well for intricate work; they are available in air- and water-soluble varieties.

Tweezers and Trolley Needle

Serger tweezers are used to hold the ribbon in place as you sew. Use the pair that came with your serger or purchase bent-nose tweezers in 5", 6", or 7" length. Choose the size that's most comfortable for you. A trolley needle also is helpful for holding the ribbon in place.

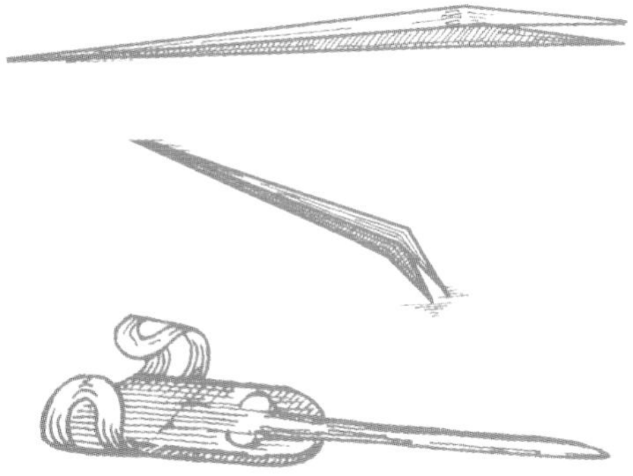

Other Fibers

Occasionally we'll mention other fibers such as pearl rayon, woolly nylon, or bouclé yarn. These are specialty fibers you can use for detail work in your embroidery. (Regular embroidery floss and crochet cotton also work well for special effects.) Treat all of these threads as if they were ribbon—don't thread them on your machine.

Helpful Hints

Follow these guidelines while stitching. Read them before you begin, and refer to them whenever you have a problem.

- Lower the presser-foot lever when you are sewing.
- Raise the presser-foot lever when you thread your sewing machine. (Note that it's harder to notice the presser-foot lever without a presser-foot attached. Try to get in the habit of lowering your presser-foot lever as soon as you put your hoop into the machine.)
- Work with your needle down in the fabric. Set your needle stop down, if you have this feature on your machine, or stop the machine with the needle in the down position.
- If you get wads of thread underneath your fabric, your presser-foot lever isn't down or your thread isn't in the tension discs. Rethread your machine and lower the presser foot.
- If your fabric bounces as you sew or the thread breaks frequently, your fabric may not be secured tightly enough in the hoop.
- If your thread breaks too often, install a new needle or try lowering your tension one more number.
- Don't worry about cutting your ribbon pieces too long. Keep a small container to hold the small pieces that are left over from the ends of a design. They'll come in handy when you need just one petal of a color or filler for a small space.
- Save your practice projects and use them to make ornaments or crazy patchwork pieces. You'll be the only one who knows they were "scraps."
- Be patient with yourself. Whenever you try a new technique, your production will be slower. Keep at it. With ribbon embroidery, the more you work, the faster and more confident you'll be.

Care of Embroidered Items

Your finished ribbon-embroidered items need special care. Most of the ribbons we've used for embroidery are machine washable and dryable—with care. Turn your garment inside out, and use a gentle washing-machine cycle. Dry on the low-temperature setting just long enough to dry; don't use high heat or overdry the garment. Of course, hand-washing and hanging to dry are completely safe for embroidered items, too.

If you're unsure about the washability of the ribbons you're using, pin them to a scrap of white fabric. Dip them in water, swish them around, and put them in the dryer. If any colors run, dry-clean the finished item and request hand-pressing to avoid smashing the ribbon embroidery.

When you press ribbon-embroidered garments yourself, press around the embroidery, not on it. If you need to press an area between two designs where the iron won't fit, try using a sleeve board. Place the embroidery just off the edge of the board to get into tight spaces.

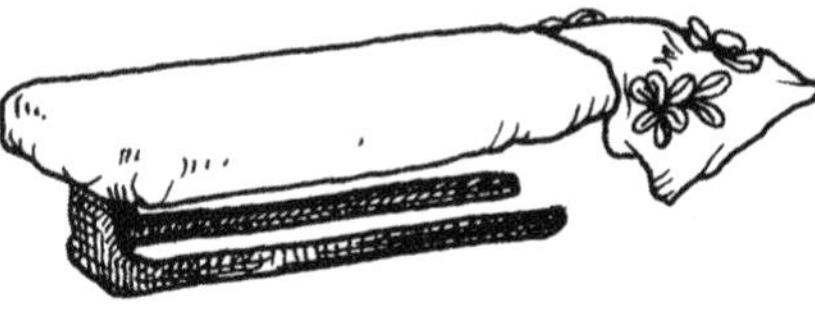

Another good way to press your finished embroidery is to place it facedown on a thick terry towel and gently steam it. The towel cushions the embroidery when you push it down.

If you have a puff iron (smockers love them), you'll find it's ideal for pressing "under" ribbon embroidery. You can press the fabric without flattening the ribbon.

If you accidentally press over some embroidery, you can fluff it back up with a burst of steam, holding the iron a few inches above the garment.

MACHINE SETUP

You can work ribbon embroidery on any sewing machine in good running condition. Take a minute to clean out any lint and to oil your machine if it normally requires oil. For ribbon embroidery, set up your sewing machine for free-motion work following these guidelines.

- Remove the presser foot and shank. If you have snap-on feet, remove the shank to which the presser foot is attached by removing the screw. Consult your machine's owner's manual for details.
- *Slowly* wind a bobbin with invisible thread—half a bobbin is plenty. Place the bobbin in your machine.
- Insert a new size 80/12 universal needle.
- Thread the needle of the machine with invisible thread with the presser foot up.
- Drop or cover the feed dogs. (Refer to the directions in your owner's manual for "sewing on a button" for the procedure for your specific machine.)
- If your machine has the option, set the needle-down feature to the down position.
- Note your normal tension setting if it's not marked on your machine. Lower the top tension by about one number.
- Engage the "slow" speed-setting feature, if you have this option.
- Make a generous sewing area by using the flat bed extension to cover your free arm.

FABRIC PREPARATION

As with any sewing project, it's important to prewash your fabric. To remove the finish and preshrink the fabric, it's usually best to wash and dry the fabric the way the finished garment will be washed and dried. When using ready-to-wear garments for ribbon embroidery—including T-shirts and sweatshirts—you

Assembling lush ribbons and fibers for ribbon embroidery is where the fun begins. Outfit your sewing area with tweezers, an air-soluble marker, scissors, and any straight-stitch sewing machine and you're ready to begin a new adventure in stitching.

also should prewash and dry the garments before sewing the embroidery.

Fabrics that won't be washed still may need pressing to remove fold creases that occurred in packaging and storage. For difficult-to-remove folds, try the steam setting or spritz the fold before pressing with one part of white vinegar to nine parts of water. If the fold line is impossible to remove, plan the placement of your embroidery design to camouflage it. You can preshrink nonwashable fabrics by steaming them lightly with an iron held slightly above the fabric. Allow the fabric to cool undisturbed lying flat on the ironing board.

FREE-MOTION STITCHING

Free-motion embroidery looks more difficult than it is. Take the time to practice on a scrap of fabric and enjoy the freedom this technique offers. Once you've mastered it, you'll wonder why you didn't learn it sooner.

First, cut an 8" square of fabric and place it in the hoop. If you do hand embroidery, note that you'll be using the hoop the opposite way. Place the larger ring of the hoop on a flat surface. Lay the fabric on top. Place the smaller ring on top, insert it in the larger ring, and tighten the screw. Pull the fabric taut. A spring hoop will tighten automatically. Thread the machine and set it up as previously instructed.

When you do free-motion stitching, you move the fabric. The sewing machine no longer feeds it for you. This enables you to move in any direction—forward, backward, or sideways. Place your hoop under the needle with the fabric against the bed of the machine, and *lower your presser foot.*

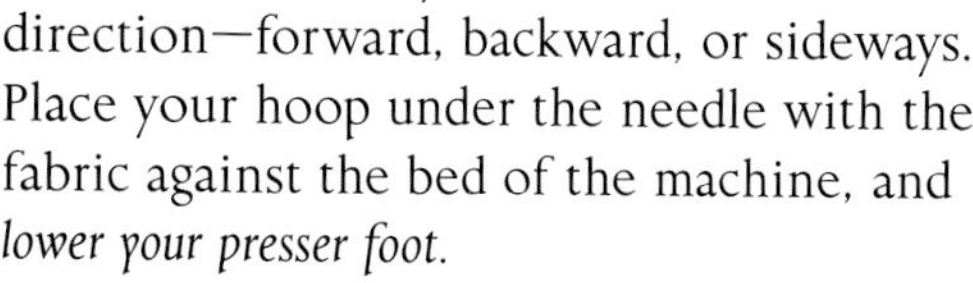

Take one stitch by manually turning the hand wheel toward you one full turn and draw the bobbin thread up so both threads are on top of the fabric. Take three or four stitches in place and snip the thread tails. Begin all of your stitching this way.

Practice moving the fabric randomly—sew sideways and backward as well as forward. Draw some circles, and practice following the lines. Keep the fabric flat against the bed of the machine while stitching; don't lift the hoop. Practice this technique until you feel comfortable with it. Then you'll be ready to start ribbon embroidery by machine.

Metallic ribbons add glitter and dazzle to the simplest of motifs. Draw holiday shapes on fabric and embellish them with metallics. Sew small pieces into pillow shapes or add piping and a hanger to make ornaments. Stuff your pieces with potpourri for sachets.

CHAPTER THREE

Stitches

No matter what endeavor you embark on, you need the basic tools and materials or ingredients, be they butter, flour, and sugar; a pencil and paper; or fabrics, patterns, thread, and a sewing machine. When you combine these ingredients in different proportions or combinations, the end result can be anything from basic white bread to an elegant cake or a pair of pull-on slacks to a bridal gown. For ribbon embroidery by machine, the individual stitches are our basic ingredients. The basic stitches are pretty by themselves, but in combination, they can be truly striking and breathtaking. And best of all, you are the creator.

BEGINNING YOUR STITCHING

Securely hold the thread coming from the needle, take one stitch through the hooped fabric, and pull the bobbin thread up to the surface. Hold the thread ends away from the needle, take a few stitches to anchor the threads, and then snip off the thread tails.

Start your ribbon embroidery in either of these ways:

- Lay out the ribbon in the direction opposite to the one in which you'll stitch. Take a few securing stitches in the ribbon end; these will be covered when the ribbon folds back on itself. Use this technique when couching, weaving, or stitching the fern stitch, lazy daisy stitch, or ribbon stitch.

OR

- Cut a 12" length of ribbon. Lay it flat on the fabric (for a smooth look) or crumple it (for a textured look), and secure it in place with a couple of machine stitches.

ENDING YOUR STITCHING

The most common way to end a stitch is to tuck the end of the ribbon under the last ribbon stitch and secure it with a few machine stitches.

When ending French knots, we like to use a knot that we call the American knot. Tie a simple overhand knot as shown and

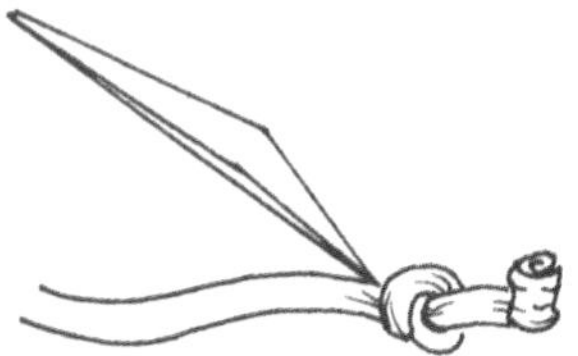

carefully nudge it up against the last French knot with your tweezers. Pull it tight and cut off the ribbon end.

When using pearl rayon thread or working French knots, you sometimes can just snip off the end of the thread or ribbon. Apply a drop or two of seam sealant to the end of the thread or ribbon to prevent fraying.

Occasionally, for a neat finish, you'll need to pull the ribbon through to the back side of the fabric. Thread the end of the ribbon onto a hand sewing needle and sew through to the back. Tie off the ribbon ends or weave them under.

MACHINE SETUP

- Remove the presser foot and shank. If you have snap-on feet, remove the shank to which the presser foot is attached by removing the screw. Consult your machine's owner's manual for details.
- *Slowly* wind a bobbin with invisible thread—half a bobbin is plenty. Place the bobbin in your machine.
- Insert a new size 80/12 universal needle.
- Thread the needle of the machine with invisible thread with the presser foot up.
- Drop or cover the feed dogs. (Refer to the directions in your owner's manual for "sewing on a button" for the procedure for your specific machine.)
- If your machine has the option, set the needle-down feature to the down position.
- Note your normal tension setting if it's not marked on your machine. Lower the top tension by about one number.
- Engage the "slow" speed-setting feature, if you have this option.
- Make a generous sewing area for your hoop by using the flat bed extension to cover your free arm.

BASIC STITCHES

There are a number of basic stitches you can use to form a variety of different shapes and flowers. Practice the basic stitches before you go on to do flowers, critters, baskets, and other projects. As you stitch, you'll no doubt develop new flowers and ideas of your own.

Chain Stitch

The chain stitch is a commonly used embroidery stitch. Use it to make roses, stems, initials, outlines, and monograms. Tweezers aren't needed for the chain stitch because you manipulate the ribbon with your hands.

1. Place the ribbon on top of the fabric and take a few stitches through the ribbon and fabric at the center of the length of ribbon.

2. Hold the ribbon out of the way of the needle, and stitch forward 1/4" onto the fabric.

3. Cross the ribbons in front of the needle. Adjust the tension on the ribbon so it's not too tight or too loose. A soft fullness is what you want. Stitch one or two stitches across the crossed ribbons.

4. Hold the ribbon out of the way of the needle and stitch forward 1/4". Again, cross the ribbons in front of the needle, and stitch. Continue repeating these steps until you've stitched the desired length.

Lazy Daisy Stitch

The lazy daisy stitch is a traditional embroidery stitch and one of the most popular. Use it to make leaves, flowers, foliage, and flower centers. As with all of the stitches, the width of the ribbon you use will determine the finished size of the stitch. The wider the ribbon, the larger the petal. Try this stitch with 2mm, 4mm, and 7mm ribbon.

1. Anchor the end of the ribbon to the fabric with a few stitches. Hold the ribbon out of the way of the needle and stitch forward 1/4", stopping with your needle down in the fabric.

2. Bring the ribbon around the needle, and anchor it with a couple of stitches. Don't pull it tight; let it lie comfortably, not too tight and not too loose. Shape the ribbon with tweezers as you sew. The ribbon should lie flat in the center and be a bit pinched at the ends.

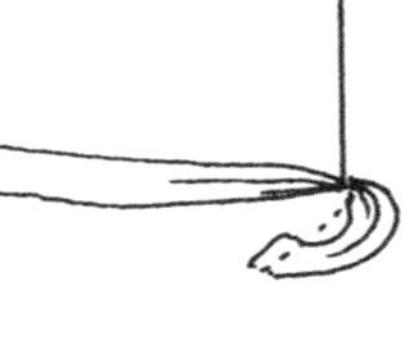

3. Then, hold the ribbon out of the way and stitch back to the starting point.

4. Carry the ribbon back to the starting point and stitch to anchor it. Again, make sure it's not too tight or too loose.

A garden trellis echoes the shape of this jacket lapel. It's filled with replicas of nature's finest small, bright flowers.

Flat Lazy Daisy Stitch

Make the flat lazy daisy stitch just like the lazy daisy stitch, but keep the ribbon flat as you stitch. Use this stitch to make iris and tulip petals.

1. Anchor the end of the ribbon. Hold the ribbon out of the way of the needle, and stitch forward 1/4" onto the fabric.

2. Keep the ribbon flat and carry it over; stitch to anchor it.

3. Stitch back to the starting point right next to the ribbon.

4. Fold the ribbon over, keeping it flat, and anchor it at the starting point. Depending on the effect you desire, you may want to pinch it a bit as you anchor it; keep the middle flat, however.

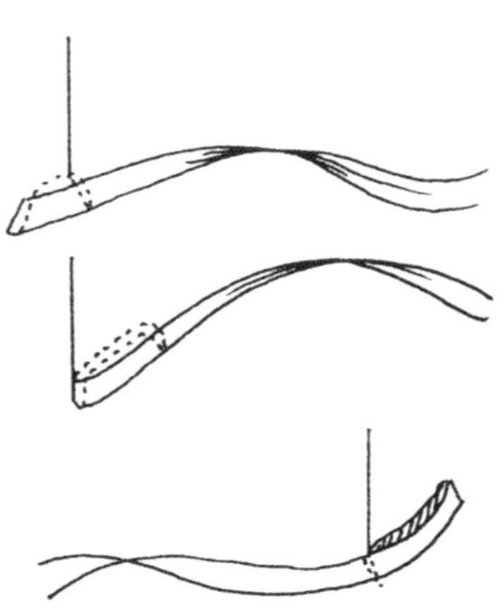

Lazy Daisy Chain Stitch

The lazy daisy chain stitch is a running lazy daisy stitch. It looks like a chain stitch but is fuller. Use this stitch in crazy quilting and to make baskets or basket handles.

1. Complete a lazy daisy stitch.

2. Stitch to the opposite end of the stitch right next to the ribbon.

3. Fold the ribbon over and anchor it.

4. Now work a second lazy daisy stitch, and repeat steps 2 and 3. Continue in this manner, making a chain of lazy daisy stitches.

Ribbon Stitch

Called a straight stitch in hand embroidery, the ribbon stitch usually is worked with 7mm ribbon. It gives the effect of a single stitch that's been pulled through the fabric. But, of course it hasn't been. For more delicate work, try working it with 4mm ribbon. The petals of this stitch are independent—not connected—making the ribbon stitch good for applications that need spaced-out stitches.

1. Pinch the end of the ribbon together and anchor it to the fabric with the end pointing toward where the petal or leaf will be.

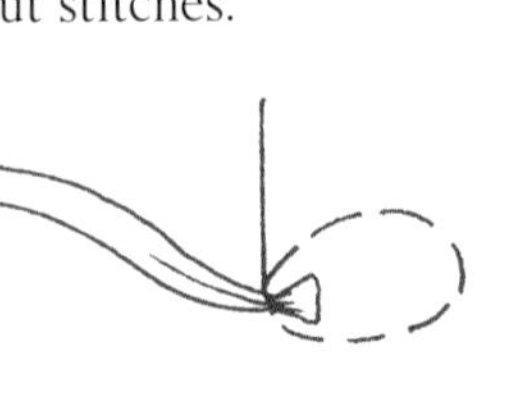

Woven ribbon hats bedecked with hatbands and roses embellish this tailored jacket.

2. Stitch 1/4" to 3/8" away to the other end of the petal or leaf.

3. Fold the ribbon over to cover the cut end. Hold the ribbon flat in the center, pinch the end, and stitch over it to anchor it. Be sure the ribbon stays flat.

4. Cut the end of the ribbon, leaving 1/4". Tuck this end under the petal, and stitch in place.

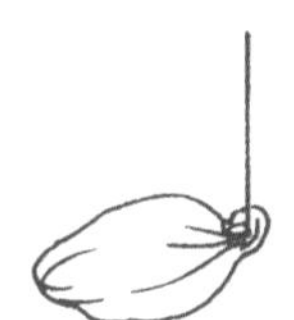

Fern Stitch

Fern stitch is the name we gave this stitch, which has a character of its own and doesn't closely resemble any traditional hand stitch. Use it to make leaves, baskets, and garden trellises. It's also good for filling in large areas.

1 Anchor the end of the ribbon, keeping it flat.

2 Hold the ribbon out of the way of the needle and stitch out 3/8" onto the fabric.

3 Place the ribbon over stitching, keeping it flat, and stitch across it to anchor it.

4 Stitch back to the other side, right next to the ribbon.

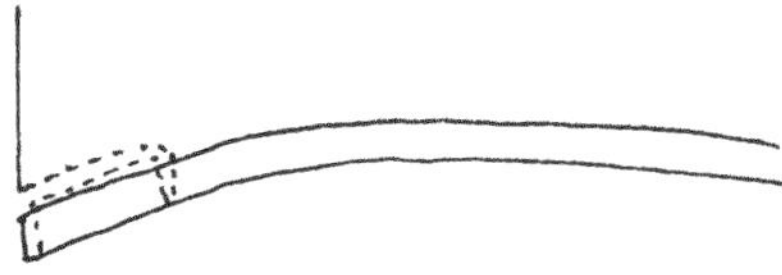

5 Fold the ribbon over again, keeping it flat, and anchor it. You want to fold it back and forth accordion-style with each turn slightly overlapping the last.

6 Stitch to the desired length and cut off the ribbon, leaving a 1/4" tail. Tuck the tail end under the last ribbon stitch, and secure it in place.

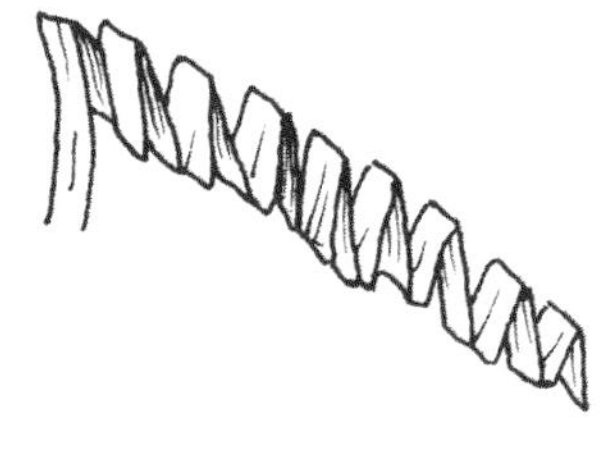

Merry little people play above these work-shirt pockets. Ask a young friend to sketch simple stick figures, then stitch them with ribbon. Add a few blossoms, grass, and some balloons to complete the scene.

French Knots

French knots are quick and easy to make. Use them wherever you want to add texture, accents, or fill. French knots often are done in clusters; try working a couple of them together.

1 Anchor the end of the ribbon to the fabric with a few stitches. With the needle down, wind the ribbon around the needle (clockwise or counterclockwise) about three times. Keep medium tension on the ribbon. The size of the French knot depends on the width of the ribbon and the number of times you wrap it around the needle.

2 Hold the wrapped ribbon in place with tweezers and stitch right outside the knot to anchor it. You may be more comfortable working this stitch by manually turning the hand wheel.

Bullion Stitch

The bullion stitch is most often used to make rosebuds. It's a variation of the French knot.

1 Start a French knot but make six wraps instead of three. After you've wrapped the ribbon, raise the needle by hand and move it slightly to one side.

2 Flip the "bullion" over on its side, and take a few stitches to secure it. Make the bud appear to be more open by spreading the ribbon a bit before taking a few stitches to secure it.

Ruching

Ruching traditionally is done by hand by gathering the ribbon down the center and then applying it to the fabric. We'll use tweezers and gather the ribbon as we go. Use ruching to make ruffly flowers and leaves.

1 Anchor the end of the ribbon to the fabric. Hold the ribbon out to the left with your left hand. With tweezers, pull about 1/4" of ribbon to the right of the needle. Take a stitch or two to anchor the ribbon and repeat.

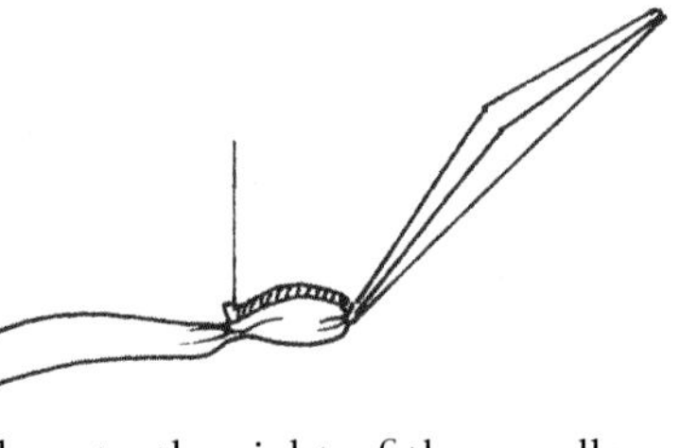

2 Continue to make a row. You can make a U-turn and double back to make the ruching wider. Tuck the tail end under and secure it in place.

Single-Edged Ruching

This variation of the ruching stitch works well for making pretty morning-glory-like flowers. Simply work ruching along just the edge of 7mm-wide ribbon.

1 Anchor the ribbon to the fabric by folding the end of the ribbon under 1/4" and stitching through all thicknesses.

2 Fold a pleat in place using your tweezers, and stitch in the center of the flower.

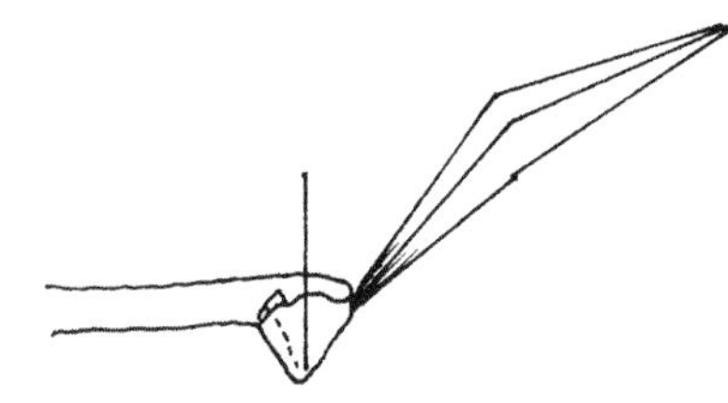

3 Continue folding pleats and stitching, working in a circle until you've completed a flower. Tuck the tail end under and secure it in place.

Loop Stitch

The loop stitch is similar to ruching. Use it to make freeform flowers of all sizes.

1 Place the ribbon on top of the fabric and take a few stitches at the end of the ribbon, stitching through both the ribbon and the fabric. Hold the ribbon in your left hand, and pull a loop to the right with your tweezers. Stitch to secure the ribbon to the fabric.

2 Continue pulling loops, working in a circle and always anchoring the loops in the same spot at the center. Tuck the tail end under the last ribbon stitch and secure it in place.

Looped Flower Variation

Work loops in rows instead of a circle to make a cascading style of flower or three-dimensional leaves and foliage.

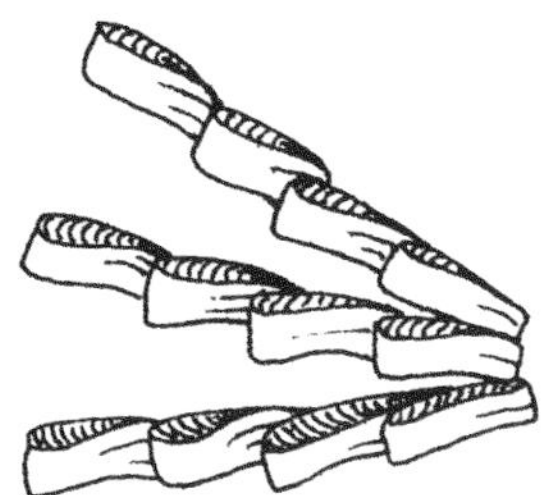

Amy's Grass

Amy needed grass for her bunny (as shown on pages 32 and 35) so she created the grass stitch using 2mm or 4mm green ribbon. You also can work grass with pearl rayon.

1. Anchor the end of the ribbon or thread, and stitch through the fabric 1/2" to 3/4" away.

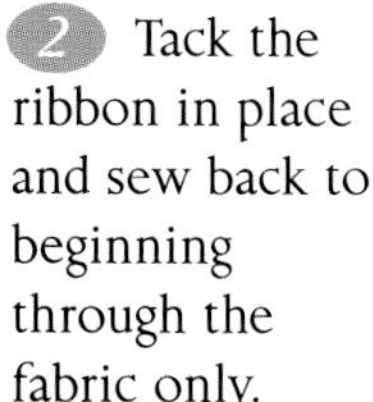

2. Tack the ribbon in place and sew back to beginning through the fabric only.

3. Fold the ribbon back on itself and tack it in place. Continue these steps. Work in clumps by coming back to the same starting point after you make each grass blade, or work a row by moving the starting point of each stitch slightly to the right of the previous stitch.

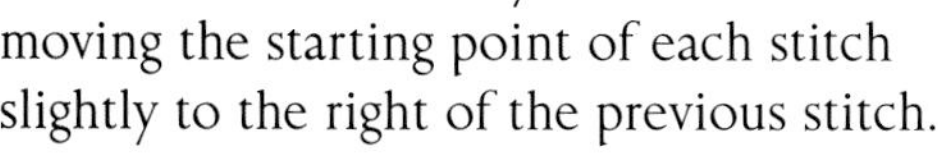

Couching

The term couching refers to tacking a surface ribbon or thread in place, as opposed to threading it into the sewing machine. In some respects, all the stitches we do could be called couching. Use couching to make stems and butterfly antennae. Try it with a variety of threads and ribbon widths.

1. Anchor the ribbon to the fabric by folding the end of the ribbon under 1/4" and stitching through all thicknesses.

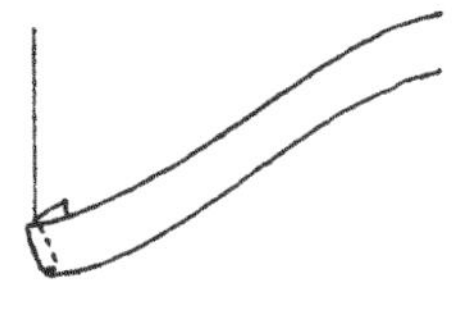

2. Stitch through the fabric only right next to the ribbon, jumping onto the ribbon at regular intervals to secure it.

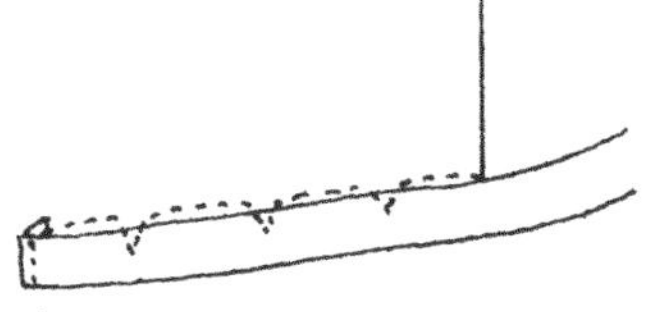

Couching with a Twist

Use this rambling stitch when you work free form or meandering designs. This stitch makes pretty script lettering on monograms, too. It's a variation of the couching stitch.

1. Anchor the ribbon to the fabric by folding the end of the ribbon under 1/4" and stitching through all thicknesses.

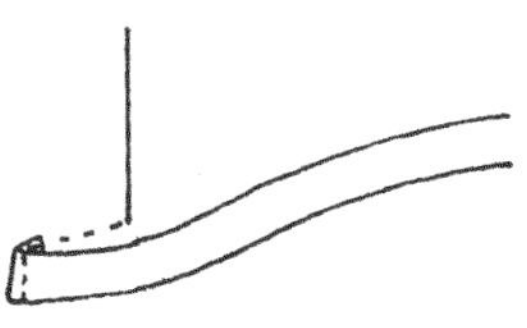

2. Twist the ribbon one half-turn. Stitch through the fabric only right next to the ribbon and secure it with a stitch where the ribbon is flat.

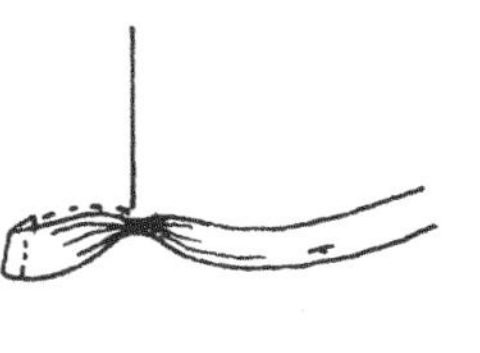

3. Continue to the desired length, following the pattern lines.

Ribbon-embroidered flowers on a fabric medallion brighten the top of a covered box. Too pretty to be tucked away, this box can sit atop a dresser or end table to hold jewelry and findings.

CHAPTER FOUR

Flowers

Ribbon-embroidered flowers are so fresh and delicate looking, you can almost smell them. Create a bed of just one type of flower or design a mixture of blooms to suit your fancy. How about a nosegay of violets, a long-stemmed rose, or a luxurious bouquet of spring blossoms? Pick and choose—you can sew one or sew them all!

Lilac

Create lilacs by stitching a cluster of French knots. Use 4mm purple ribbons for the blossoms and 4mm green ribbon for the stems and leaves.

1. Choose three shades of purple, and work with the trio of threads to make French knots in irregularly sized clusters. No need to cut the ribbons between the French knots; instead, space the knots closely and carry the ribbons between your stitches.

2. Work chain-stitch stems and lazy daisy leaves with green ribbon.

Tulip

Make tulips in lively colors—reds, yellows, and bright fuchsias—with vertical lazy daisy stitches. Use either 4mm or 7mm ribbon for the blossoms, 4mm ribbon for the stems, and 4mm or 7mm ribbon for the leaves. You'll probably want to use the same ribbon size for the blossoms and the leaves.

1. Make one vertical lazy daisy stitch.

2. Work two more lazy daisy stitches at 45-degree angles to the first one. Slightly overlap these two stitches at the bottom. Cut the ribbon and tuck it under. If you're stitching several tulips close together in a cluster, make all of the heads first, then continue with the leaves and stems.

3 Anchor the stem ribbon at the bottom of the tulip as you did for the ribbon stitch. Keep the ribbon flat, and stitch through the fabric only to the bottom of the stem. Lay the ribbon next to the stitching, and stitch across the stem base to secure the ribbon.

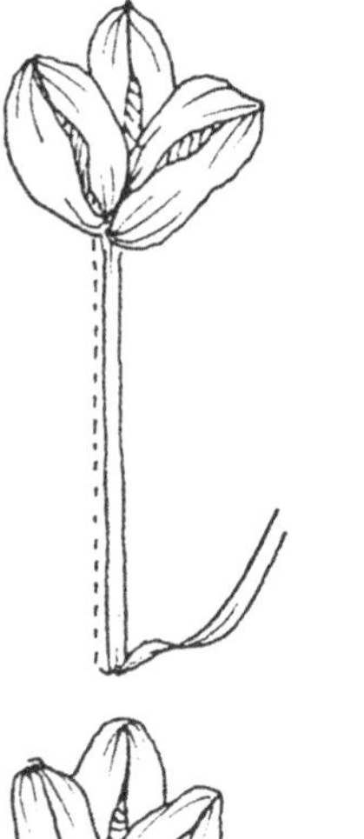

4 To make the leaves, anchor the ribbon at the stem if you're using a different size ribbon for your leaves. Otherwise, continue with the same ribbon. Keep the ribbon flat, and stitch through the fabric only to the tip of the leaf. Stitch across the ribbon at the top. Stitch back to the bottom of the stem next to the ribbon and through the fabric only.

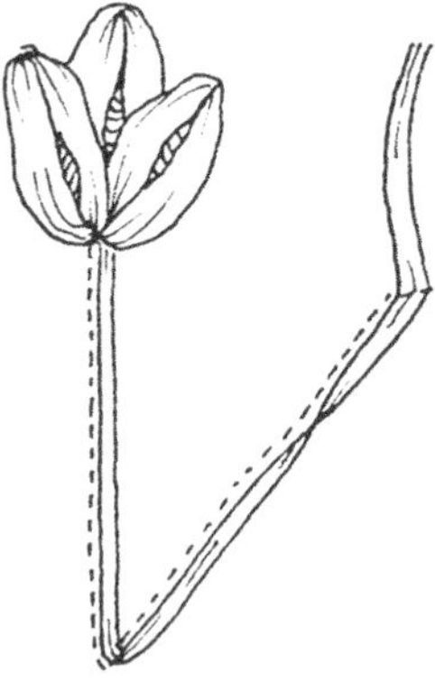

5 Fold the ribbon back on itself, keeping it flat or adding a half-twist. Stitch across the ribbon at the leaf-stem base. Repeat for the second leaf.

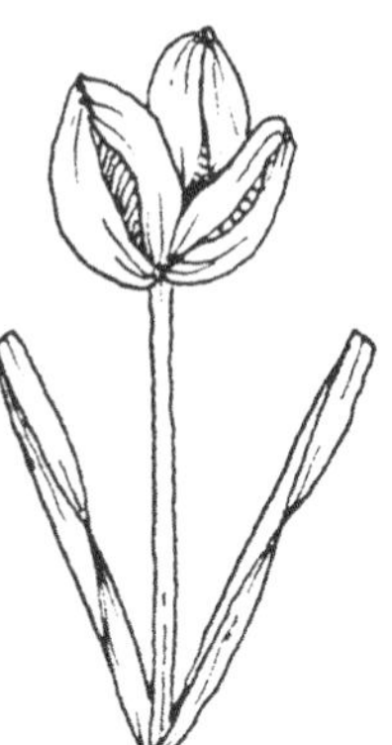

Iris

Real irises come in almost every color of the rainbow. Choose several shades of a single color or combine two shades of one hue with a contrasting color. Use either 4mm or 7mm ribbon for the blooms, stitch the stems with 4mm green ribbon, and work the leaves with 4mm or 7mm ribbon.

1 With the lightest shade of ribbon, work a vertical lazy daisy stitch at the center of the area designated for the bloom. Cut the ribbon and tuck the end under.

2 With a darker shade of the same color, work two lazy daisy stitches pointing down at 45-degree angles from the base of the first stitch. Cut the ribbon and tuck the end under.

3 With the darkest or contrasting shade of ribbon, work a French knot at the centers of the lazy daisy stitches. Add the stems and leaves as you did for the tulip.

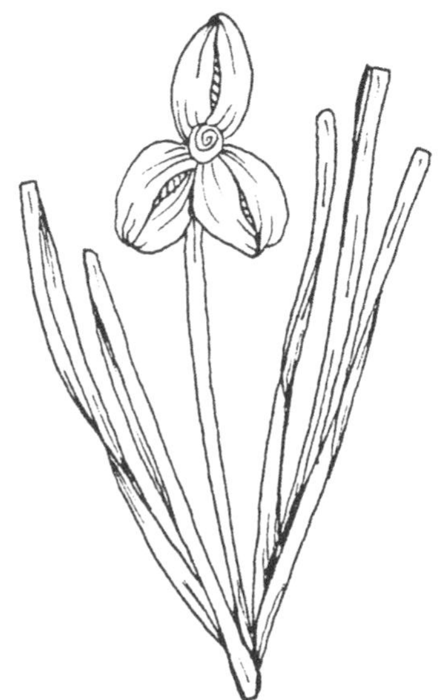

A purchased or handmade fleece pullover and hat are personalized with a few favorite flowers.

Daffodil

Use shades of yellow and white ribbons in 4mm or 7mm sizes for daffodils. Stitch the stems with 4mm green ribbon and the leaves with 4mm or 7mm ribbon.

1. Work a vertical lazy daisy stitch at the center of the area designated for the bloom. Don't cut the ribbon. Stitch through the fabric only to the top of the vertical lazy daisy stitch.

2. Fold the ribbon over to the top of the vertical lazy daisy stitch, and take several stitches to secure it. Work two or three French knots, then cut the ribbon and tuck the end under.

3. With a different shade of ribbon at the bottom of the first lazy daisy stitch, work three or four lazy daisies that point down. Add stems and leaves as you did for the tulip.

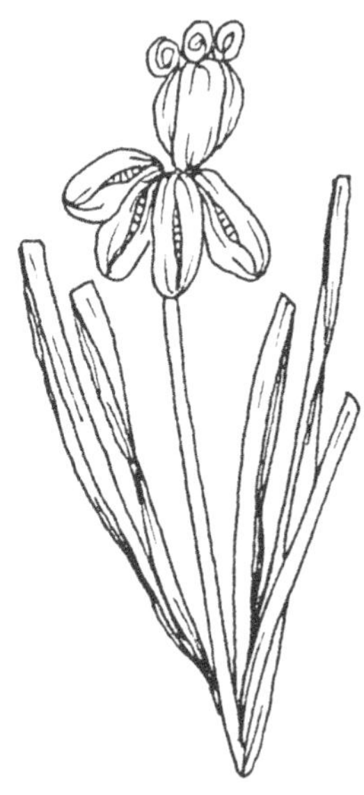

Chain-Stitch Rose

Use pink, white, cream, yellow, salmon, or red ribbon to make realistic roses. Work with a 12" to 15" length of 4mm or 7mm ribbon; the 7mm size makes an especially luxurious bloom.

1 Draw three dots in a triangle about 1/4" apart. Precision isn't important; the dot layout is the same for a small bud or a large rose.

2 Place the center of the ribbon over any dot, and take three or four stitches to anchor it in place.

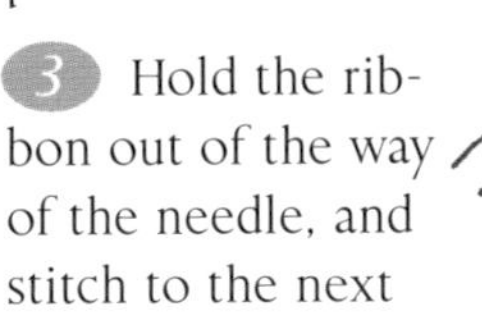

3 Hold the ribbon out of the way of the needle, and stitch to the next dot.

4 Cross the ribbons in front of the needle. Adjust the tension on the ribbon so it's not too tight or too loose; a soft fullness is what you want. Take one or two stitches across the crossed ribbons.

5 Hold the ribbon out of the way of the needle, and stitch to the last dot. Again, cross the ribbons in front of the needle and stitch across them, continuing a few stitches beyond the first dot. This makes the first round of the rose.

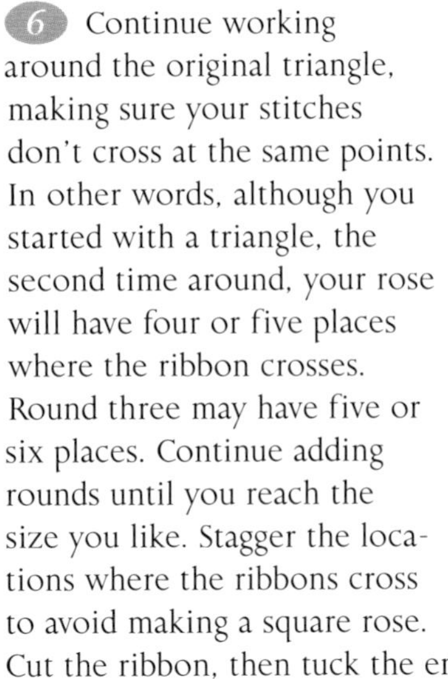

6 Continue working around the original triangle, making sure your stitches don't cross at the same points. In other words, although you started with a triangle, the second time around, your rose will have four or five places where the ribbon crosses. Round three may have five or six places. Continue adding rounds until you reach the size you like. Stagger the locations where the ribbons cross to avoid making a square rose. Cut the ribbon, then tuck the end under and secure it in place.

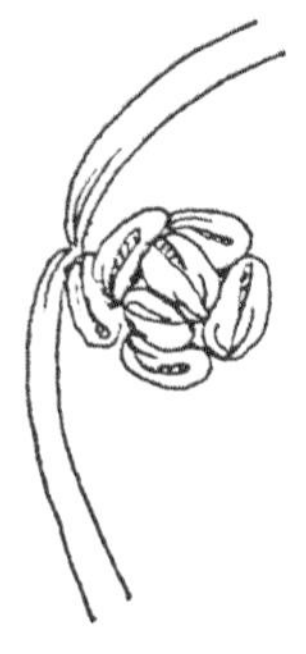

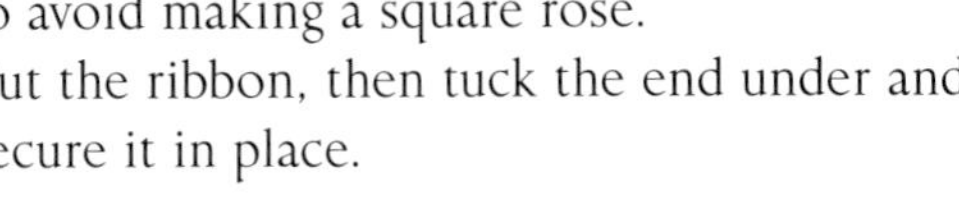

Shaded Chain-Stitch Rose

Make shaded or multicolored roses by stitching a chain-stitch rose with two shades of a single color of ribbon. The two colors intertwine for an unusual effect. Cut a 6" length of *two* different shades of ribbon. Overlap one end of each ribbon and take three or four stitches across the overlap to secure them.

1 Draw dots as you did for the chain-stitch rose.

2 Stitch as you did for the chain-stitch rose.

A basket-weave cameo surrounded by flowers and leaves elevates the common T-shirt to an elegant wearable.

Oval Rose

Make these roses with a cluster of chain stitches. Use either 4mm or 7mm ribbon in red, pink, yellow, or white for each rose; use green for the stems and leaves. Work with a 12" to 15" length of ribbon to make the bloom.

1 Work two consecutive chain stitches in a row.

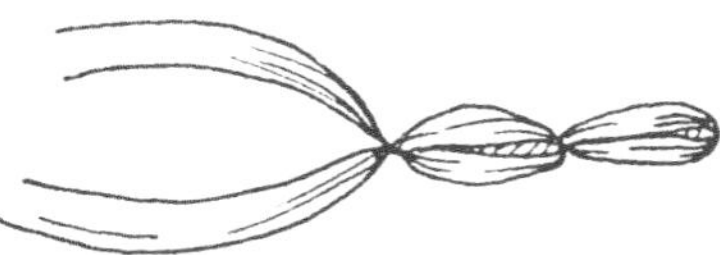

2 Change direction and work more chain stitches in an overall oval shape. Continue adding rounds to the oval until you reach the size you like. Stagger the positions of the stitches to avoid making the rose symmetrical. Cut the ribbon, tuck the end under, and secure it in place.

3 To make a rose in profile, add a few green lazy daisy stitches at the bottom of the rose.

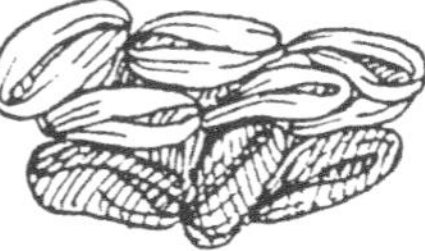

Sunflower

Choose nature's sunniest yellows to make sunflowers. Use 4mm or 7mm yellow ribbon for the flowers, 4mm dark-brown or black ribbon for the centers, and 4mm green ribbon for the stems and leaves.

1 Draw a 1" to 1 1/2" circle, and work a circle of lazy daisy stitches around it.

2 Fill the center with French knots.

3 Couch a strong, tall stem starting at the stem bottom and ending under a flower petal. Cut the ribbon, tuck the end under, and secure it in place. Work the lazy-daisy-stitch leaves.

For a double sunflower, make the lazy daisy circle as described above. Work a random row of looped-flower-variation petals overlapping the lazy daisy stitches. Let the looped flowers droop as real sunflowers do.

Lazy Daisy Flower

Daisies commonly have white or yellow petals; choose either color in 4mm ribbon to make the flowers. Use 4mm green ribbon for the stems and leaves.

1 Make a dot on the fabric and form a circle of eight dots around it. Anchor the end of the ribbon at the center dot.

2 Work a lazy daisy stitch from the center out to any dot.

3 Continue working lazy daisy stitches around the circle until the flower is complete. The direction or sequence of your stitching isn't important.

4 Fill in the center with three or four French knots.

5 Anchor the ribbon for the stem at the mid-point between two petals near the center of the flower. Work a chain-stitch stem, adding a curve for realism.

6 Stop where you'd like to add leaves and work several lazy daisy leaves with *one* of the ribbons, then continue the chain-stitch stem with both ribbons. Thread the ribbon tails on a hand needle, pull them to the back side of the fabric, and tie them off or tuck them under.

Chrysanthemum

Choose 2mm or 4mm ribbon in a single color or in two shades of the same fall-tone hue to work a lifelike mum.

1 Make a 1" to 1 1/2" circle with an air-soluble marker. Beginning at the outside of the circle, work lazy daisy stitches. If you're using two shades of ribbon, carry both along and work with them at the same time. Make a couple of stitches with one shade, then work a stitch or two with the second shade.

2 Continue working around the outside of the circle until it's filled.

3 Start the next row 1/4" in toward the center, overlapping the first row about halfway. Continue until the circle is filled.

Peony

Graceful pink peonies are one of nature's prettiest specimens. Make peony blooms with 7mm ribbon in any color you like. Use 2mm or 4mm green ribbon for the stems and 4mm ribbon for the leaves.

A peony is sewn much like a mum except that it's stitched in rows worked from the top down instead of in a circle.

1 Draw a 1" to $1^{1}/_{2}$" circle with an air-soluble marker. Beginning at the top of the circle, work a row of lazy daisy stitches about an inch long.

2 Directly below the last stitch of the first row, begin to stitch your way back across, overlapping the first row slightly. The tops of the lazy daisy stitches in the second row will just cover the bottoms of the stitches in the first row.

3 Work your way down the circle, working a couple fewer stitches in each successive row and just three or four stitches in the last row.

4 Work several lazy daisy stitches in green at the base of the flower and continue down with a couched stem and more lazy daisy leaves.

Fern

Choose 4mm ribbon in green to make ferns. For leaves that are true to nature, remember that tender, young ferns that have had little exposure to light actually are light to medium yellow-green; mature ferns range from medium to dark green or blue-green.

1 Draw a rough outline of a fern with an air-soluble marker. Accuracy isn't important.

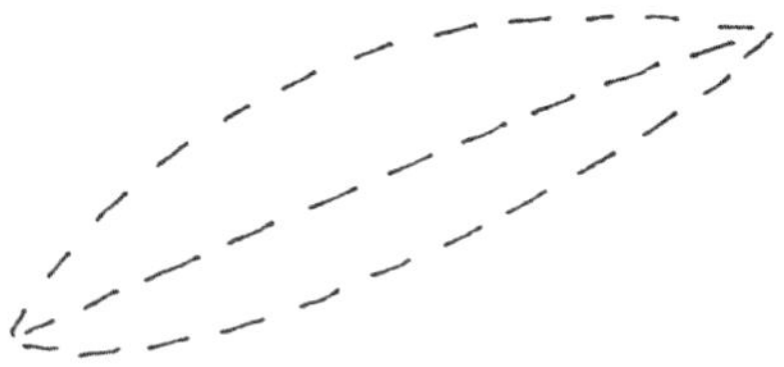

2 Anchor the end of the ribbon at the bottom center of the leaf.

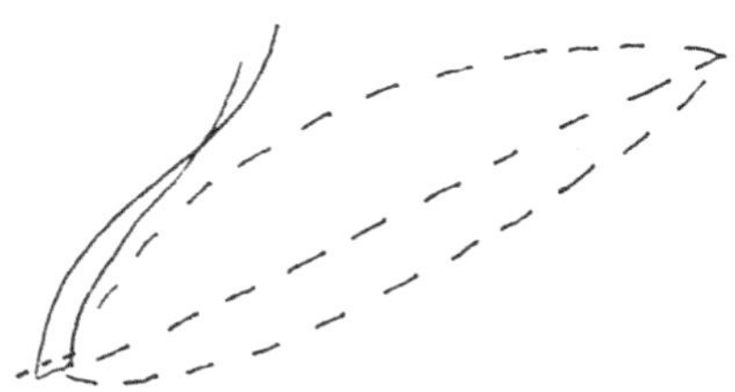

3 Work fern stitches to cover the first half of the leaf.

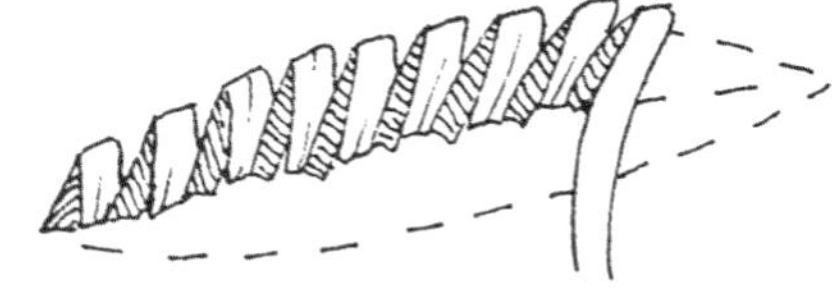

4 As you approach the tip of the leaf, fan out your stitches as shown.

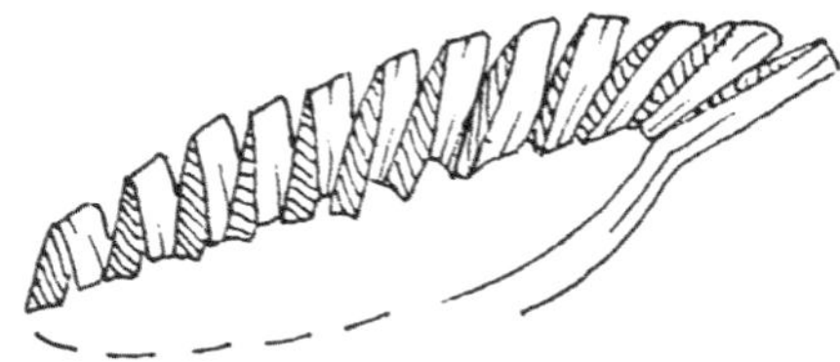

5 Work your way down the opposite side, being certain to overlap your first rows slightly to avoid a gap down the center of the leaf. If your completed leaf does have a gap, work chain stitches up the center to cover it.

Holiday greenery and ribbons make this blouse one you'll want to wear all winter long.

Pinecone

Choose 4mm brown ribbon to make the cones and green pearl rayon thread for the stems and leaves.

1 Draw an oval shape with an air-soluble marker to represent the pinecone. Turn your hoop so the pinecone is sitting on the side of the oval. Using 4mm ribbon, begin at the top, which will be the small part, and sew a horizontal row of fern stitches.

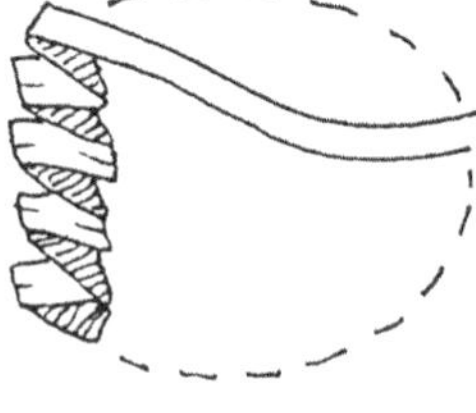

2 Stitch another row of fern stitches directly below, staggering them and slightly overlapping the first row.

3 Continue in the same manner until the pinecone is complete. Add a chain-stitch stem and, using green pearl rayon, work some elongated lazy daisy stitches for a pine branch. If you prefer, work evergreens with a feather stitch using 2mm ribbon (see page 147). Sew the feather stitches close together and make them of random length.

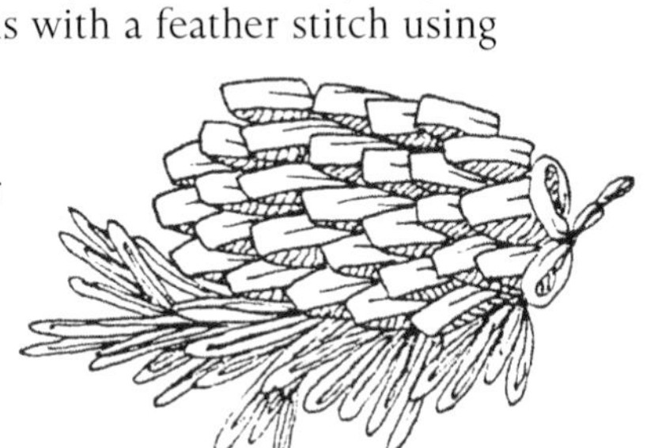

Bullion Rosebud

Bullion rosebuds are a welcome addition to any bouquet. Make the bud center with 7mm pink, red, white, or yellow ribbon and the leaves with 7mm green ribbon.

1 Work a bullion stitch using 7mm ribbon. As you anchor the ribbon at the end, fold it over as shown and stitch it in place.

2 Work one or two lazy daisy stitches with green ribbon at the base of the bud, covering the cut end of the bullion stitch.

Ruched Flowers

Clusters of ruched flowers can fill the empty spaces around other flowers and leaves. Work basic ruching wherever you need flowers to fill a design. Try ruching two intertwining shades of the same color. By intertwining green with the flower color, you get the effect of a vine among the flowers. Use 4mm or 7mm ribbon for the flowers and 4mm ribbon for the intertwining vine and flowers.

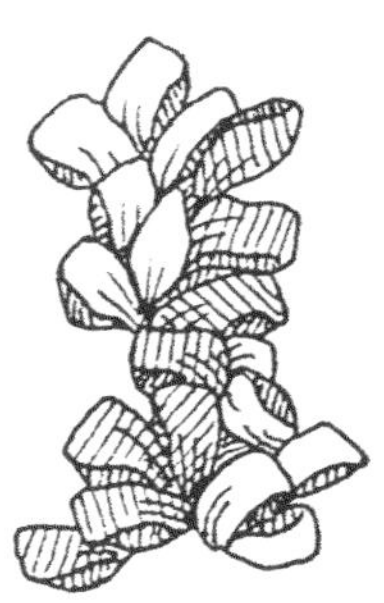

Looped Flowers

Make these casual, field-type flowers using 2mm or 4mm ribbon for the blooms and 2mm or 4mm ribbon for the stems and leaves. Use 2mm ribbon for small, delicate flowers and 7mm ribbon for large, luxurious blooms.

1. Work a loop stitch using 2mm or 4mm ribbon. Work from the center of the flower, pulling loops out to the side as you go.

2. Work a few French knots at the center of the flower.

3. Work a chain-stitch stem with 2mm or 4mm ribbon, and lazy daisy or ribbon-stitch leaves with 4mm or 7mm ribbon.

Cascading Loop Flowers

Create flowing vines of flowers and leaves with rows of loop stitches. Try working the flowers with 2mm or 4mm ribbon in several shades of the same color along with a shade or two of 4mm green ribbon for the leaves.

1 Turn the hoop so the top of the first flower is to the right. Working right to left, work a single loop stitch with a second loop stitch just to the left of it.

2 Repeat four or five times.

3 Work varying-length rows of loop stitches to complete the blossoms.

4 Work leaves of loop stitches or lazy daisy stitches at the bases of the blossoms.

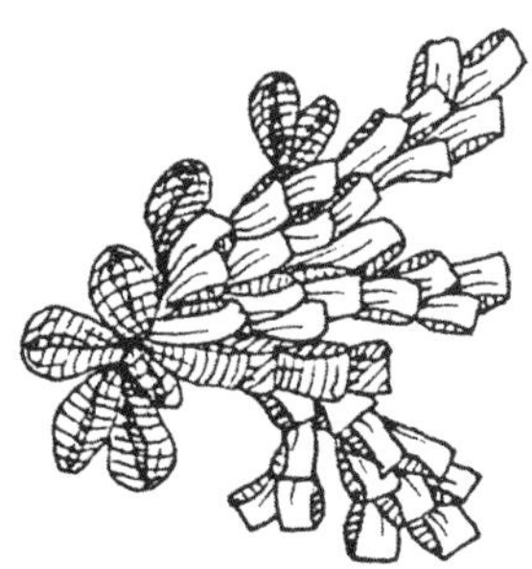

Bluebell

Spring's bluebells add a touch of life and a unique splash of color to the mixed flower garden. Make both blooms and leaves of 4mm or 7mm ribbon.

1 Make a lazy daisy stitch for the first bluebell. Cut the ribbon, move to the next flower, and repeat. Continue making bluebells about 1/4" or 1/2" apart until you achieve the desired overall size.

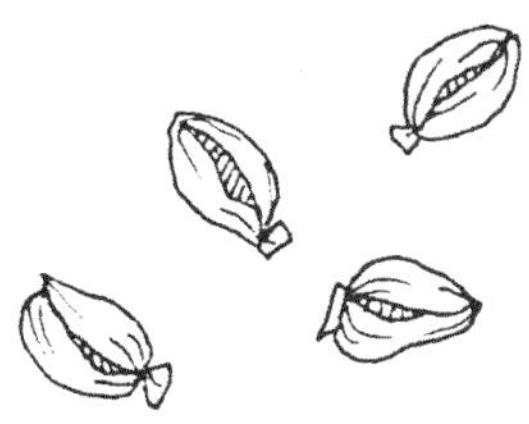

2 Anchor green ribbon below the first lazy daisy stitch and work lazy daisy leaves on each side of the first bluebell, making certain to cover the cut ends of the blue ribbon.

3 Stitch to the next bluebell, keeping the ribbon out of the way. Then bring in the green ribbon at the base of this bluebell and anchor it. Sew lazy daisy leaves around this flower.

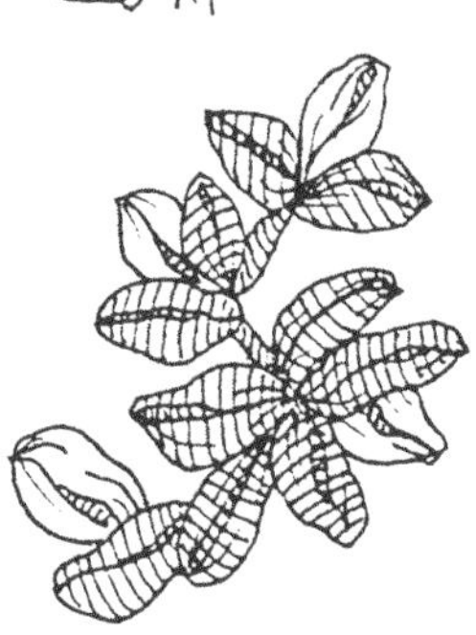

4 Work more lazy daisy leaves that extend to the next bluebell, and repeat steps 2 and 3.

5 Fill the area where the bluebell joins the leaves with a contrasting-color French knot, if desired.

Ribbon-Stitch Flowers

Use ribbon stitches to make a variety of flowers. Because each petal is stitched independently, 7mm ribbon works well. But for a delicate look, you can use 4mm ribbon. Use 2mm or 4mm ribbon for the stems.

1 Draw a small circle with an air-soluble marker. Work an uneven number of independent ribbon stitches around the circle. Remember—to work one stitch, cut the ribbon and then start the next.

2 Fill in the center of the flower with French knots. For variety, stitch a 2mm small lazy daisy stitch on top of each ribbon stitch.

3 Anchor the ribbon for the stem at the midpoint between two petals near the center of the flower. Work a chain-stitch stem and lazy daisy or ribbon-stitch leaves.

Pansy

Fresh-faced pansies are a delight in any sunny garden. Or use contrasting shades of 7mm purple ribbon for the flowers, 2mm or 4mm yellow ribbon for the centers, and black pearl cotton for accents.

1 Draw a shallow oval shape with an air-soluble marker. Work three ribbon stitches at the bottom of the oval.

2 Make two ribbon stitches with a contrasting shade of ribbon at the top of the oval.

3 Using heavy black pearl cotton or crochet thread, work a lazy daisy stitch at the center of each ribbon stitch. End each lazy daisy stitch with a French knot.

4 Fill in the center of the pansy with two yellow French knots.

Dandelion

Although you slave to keep dandelions out of your garden, there are times when you'll want to stitch one. Use 2mm yellow ribbon for the flower heads and 2mm green ribbon for the leaves and stems. The unique leaf—smooth on one side and jagged on the other—also works well for marigolds, mums, and poppies.

1 Work three or four yellow lazy daisy stitches in a row at the top of the dandelion.

2 Directly below the last stitch of the first row, begin to stitch your way across, making six or seven lazy daisy stitches that slightly overlap the first row.

3 Work one or two more rows to complete the flower head.

4 Work the stem by couching a 2mm ribbon in place. Anchor a 4mm ribbon slightly above the base of the stem.

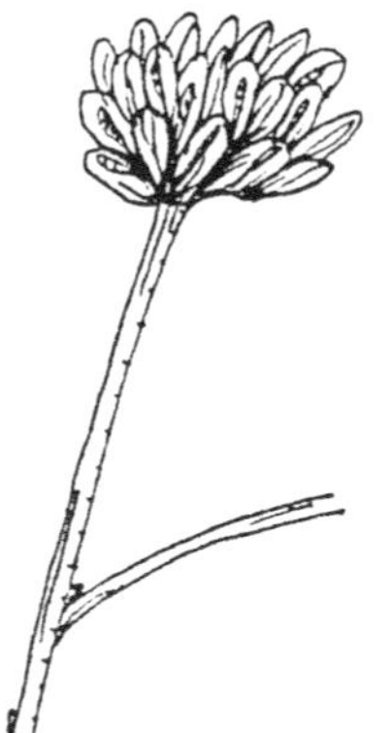

5 Work one long lazy daisy stitch the whole length of the leaf. The ribbon is now back at the base of the leaf.

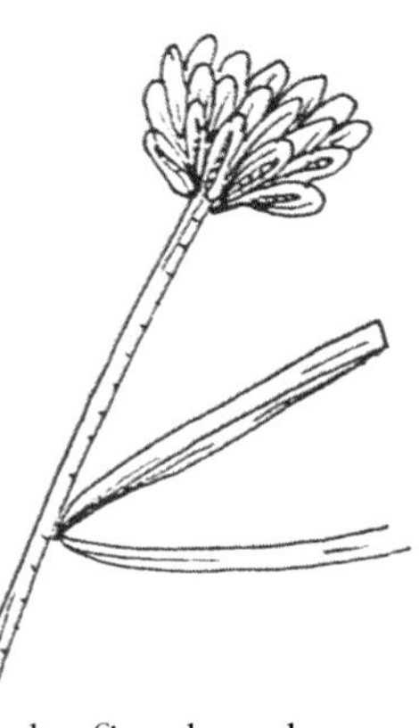

6 Work a series of shorter lazy daisy stitches of varying length to one side of the long stitch. Each of the shorter stitches will slightly overlap the first long lazy daisy stitch.

Morning Glory

Flowing vines of colorful morning glories are beautiful whether climbing a trellis or flowing from a garland. Use 7mm white or pale pastel ribbon for the flowers and buds, 2mm yellow ribbon for the flower centers, 2mm green ribbon or pearl rayon thread for the stems, and 7mm green ribbon for the leaves.

1 Draw the stem and its offshoots with an air-soluble marker. Work a meandering chain-stitch stem over your drawing with 2mm ribbon or pearl rayon thread.

2 Work morning-glory flowers with a single-edged ruching stitch on the stem.

3 Work some partially open buds by stitching one-half of a single-edged ruching flower. Stitch one or two green-ribbon lazy daisy stitches at the base of each flower.

4 Stitch a small French knot at the center of the open flower with 2mm ribbon or pearl cotton. Add 7mm green leaves in ribbon stitches.

Carnation

Cheery carnations are the florist's staple. Make them with 7mm ribbon in two shades of just about any color of the rainbow. Use 4mm green ribbon for the leaves and stems.

1 Work carnations by stitching half of a single-edged ruching flower.

1 Just below the first stitching, work a second half-single-edged ruching flower in a slightly lighter color of

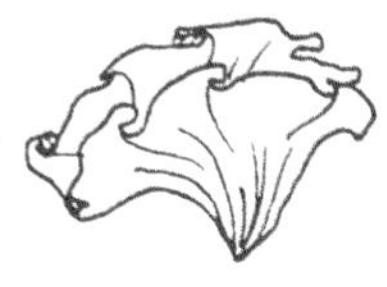

ribbon. The first should just peek out above the second.

3 Work green lazy daisy stitches at the base of the flower. Stitch a chain-stitch stem with irregular lazy daisy leaves.

Violet

Whether you're making a bouquet or a woodland scene, it isn't complete without violets. Choose a variety of shades of 4mm or 7mm purple, blue, yellow, or white ribbon for the flowers; 4mm green ribbon for the leaves; and green pearl rayon for the stems.

1 Draw a small circle with an air-soluble marker. Work five or six 7mm ribbon stitches or 4mm lazy daisy stitches around the perimeter of the circle.

2 For variety, work some flowers with two petals of one shade and three of a lighter one.

3 Work one or two French knots with yellow ribbon at each flower center.

4 For a side view or profile of violets, work all stitches on one side, varying dark and light shades.

5 Work a chain-stitch stem with green pearl rayon. Work individual 7mm ribbon-stitch leaves on each side of the stem.

Geranium

When Memorial Day arrives, official geranium-planting season begins. Stitch the blossoms in 4mm or 7mm pink, coral, red, or white ribbon; the stems in 2mm green ribbon; and the leaves in 7mm dark-green ribbon.

1 Work a cluster of French knots with 4mm or 7mm ribbon.

2 Couch a straight stem with 2mm green ribbon.

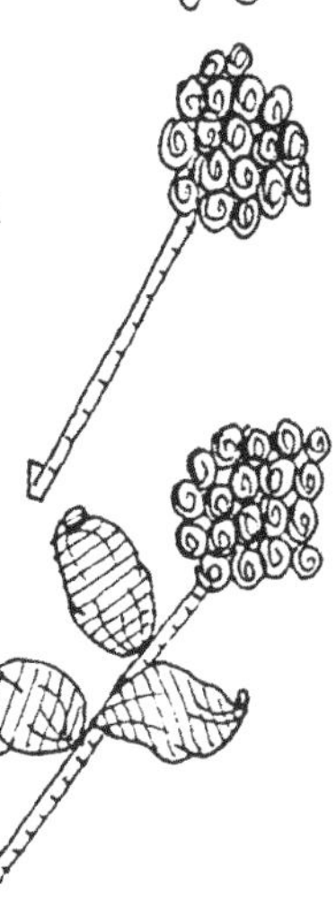

3 Work individual 7mm ribbon-stitch leaves on each side of the stem.

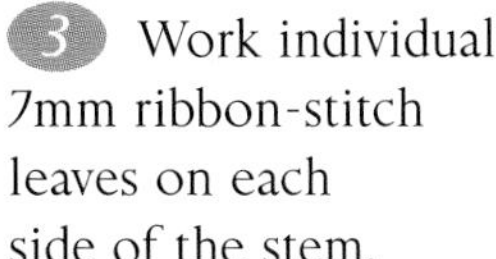

Thistle

The thistle, Scotland's well-known contribution to the floral world, is prickly and "pokey" by nature. To achieve this look, do much of your work with pearl rayon or a similar thread. Use 2mm pink, white, or lavender ribbon for the thistle flowers and green pearl rayon for the leaves and stems.

1 Draw a shallow arc with an air-soluble marker to represent the top of the thistle flower. Work a row of four or five elongated lazy daisy stitches to cover the arc.

2 Work another row of seven or eight lazy daisy stitches directly below and slightly overlapping the first row.

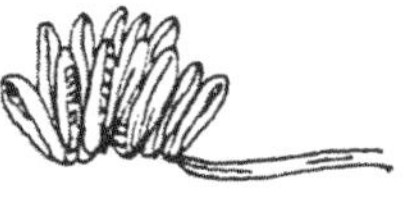

3 Continue adding rows of stitches in this manner until you achieve the desired size. The thistle flower should have a rounded shape.

4 Work a variety of sizes of lazy daisy stitches at the base of the thistle flower using green pearl rayon.

5 Couch a straight stem of green pearl rayon, and sew back up at an angle to form the spine of the leaf.

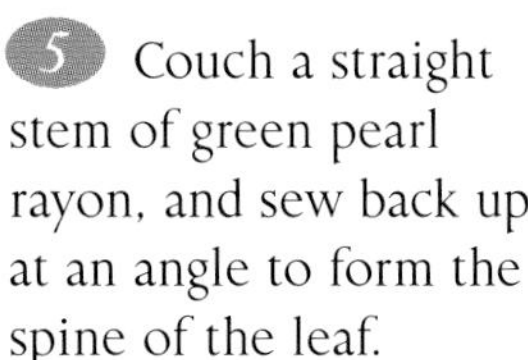

6 Work a variety of sizes of elongated lazy daisy stitches to create a leaf that radiates from the spine.

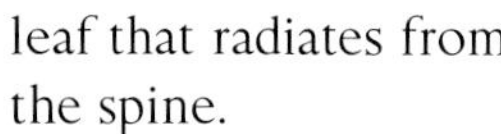

7 Work stitches around the tip of the leaf and back down the opposite side. Couch the second leaf spine and the rest of the stem. Work elongated lazy daisy stitches on both sides of the second spine as you did previously.

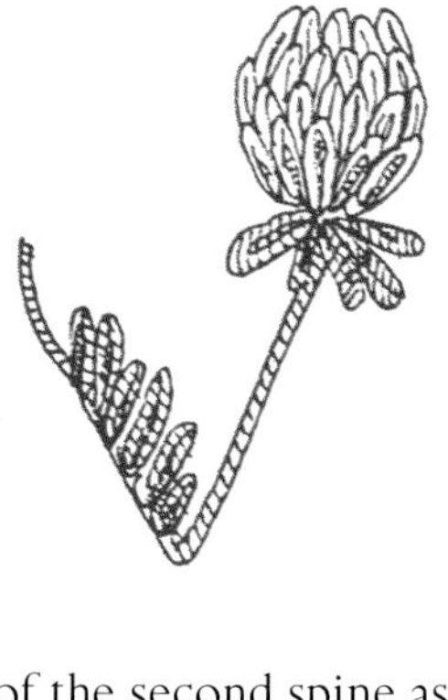

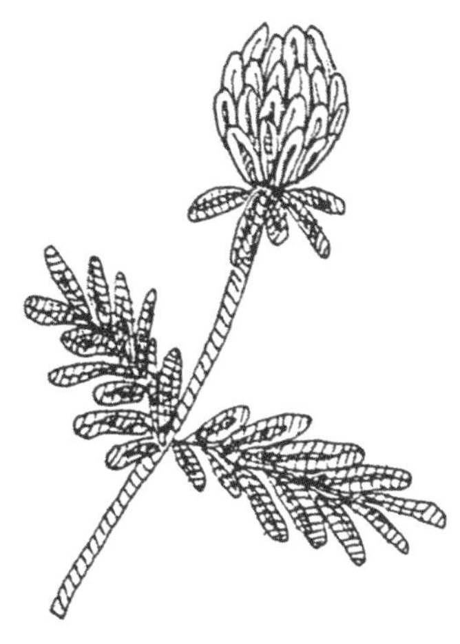

Judy's Mum

We love ribbon embroidery because you never know what will develop as you sew. During one of our classes, Judy Sieberg was making a mum. She didn't like the way it was developing so she added looped stitches in the center. It was sensational! Here's how she did it with 4mm ribbon.

1 Draw a 1" to $1^{1}/_{2}$" circle with an air-soluble marker. Beginning outside the circle

as you did for the chrysanthemum, work a round of lazy daisy stitches, leaving a hole at the center.

2 Fill the center with loop stitches, continuing to work in concentric circles until the center is filled.

Bachelor's Button

Bachelor's buttons usually come in shades of lavender, blue, pink, and white. In real or stitched bouquets, they make excellent filler flowers. Choose 2mm ribbon for the flowers, stems, and leaves.

1 Draw a 1/2"- to 1"-diameter circle with an air-soluble marker. Beginning outside the circle, work loop stitches with the loops 1/4" to 3/8" long around the entire perimeter of the circle.

2 Start the next row about 1/4" in toward the center, overlapping the first row about halfway. Continue until the circle is completely filled. Fold the ribbon end under and tack it in place.

3 Anchor 2mm ribbon for the stem at the midpoint between any two flower petals. Work a chain-stitch stem, adding a curve for realism. Stop where you'd like to add leaves and work several feathery fern leaves with one of the ribbons. Then continue the chain-stitch stem with both ribbons. Thread the ribbon tails on a hand needle, pull them to the back side of the fabric, and tie them off.

Cattail

Every roadside stream grows cattails in abundance. Use these perennial favorites wherever you want a fall look. Use 7mm brown ribbon for the cattails, 2mm green ribbon or pearl rayon for the stems, and 4mm green ribbon for the leaves.

1 Draw a line to represent the stem with an air-soluble marker. Couch a length of 2mm green ribbon in place for the stem or work chain stitches with green pearl rayon.

2 Work a brown bullion stitch near the top of the stem.

3 Anchor the leaf ribbon at the base of the stem. Keep the ribbon flat and stitch through the fabric only to the tip of the leaf. Stitch across the ribbon at the top. Stitch back to the bottom of the stem next to the ribbon through the fabric only.

4 Fold the ribbon back on itself, keeping it flat or adding a half-twist. Stitch across the ribbon at the leaf-stem base. Repeat for the second leaf.

Calla Lily

Graceful lilies grow in white and shades of yellow and pink. Use 7mm ribbon for the blooms, 2mm yellow ribbon for the flower centers, 2mm green ribbon or pearl rayon thread for the stems, and 7mm green ribbon for the leaves. The calla lily worked in 2mm or 4mm ribbon without a center also makes a good rosebud.

1 Fold the 7mm bloom ribbon in half and stitch it in place at the base of the flower.

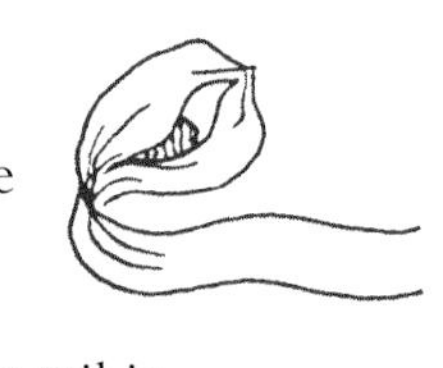

2 Fold the ribbon as shown, bringing the end around the needle while holding the flower in place, and stitch it at the base. Cut the ribbon, tuck it under, and stitch the tail in place.

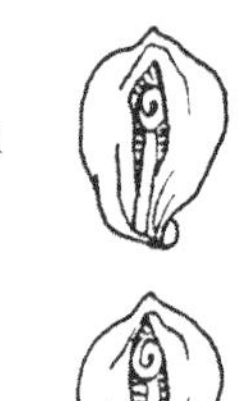

3 Couch the yellow ribbon from the base of the flower halfway up inside the center fold. Work a French knot at the end of the couching.

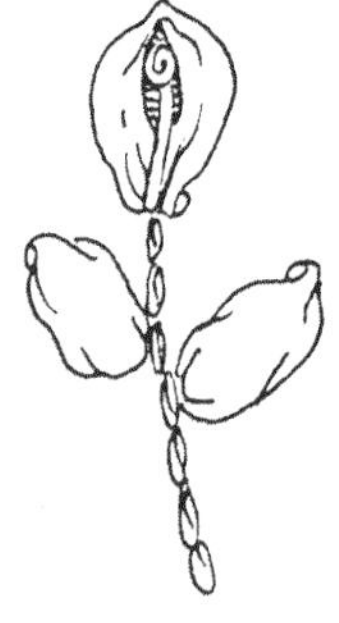

4 Work a chain-stitch stem with 2mm green ribbon or pearl cotton. Work ribbon-stitch leaves with 7mm green ribbon.

Those who eagerly await the first signs of spring will appreciate this garden scene. What says it better than a white picket fence and trellis bedecked with Mother Nature's best? The bunny is created from fake fur.

CHAPTER FIVE

Garden Containers

Display your ribbon-embroidered flowers in charming baskets and flowerpots, or "plant" them along a picket fence or climbing up a trellis.

Trellis

A stitched trellis is more than just a structure for climbing flowers; you can use it to make a flower box, a window box, or an interesting garden background. Use 2mm, 4mm or 7mm ribbon to make a trellis.

1 Begin by drawing rows of dots about 1/2" to 3/4" apart, as shown. We show three rows of dots for a double trellis, but you can make two rows for a single trellis or multiple rows for an even larger trellis.

Hint: Remember, always stitch first then follow with the ribbon.

2 Lay the end of the ribbon on dot A, as shown. Stitch to anchor the cut end.

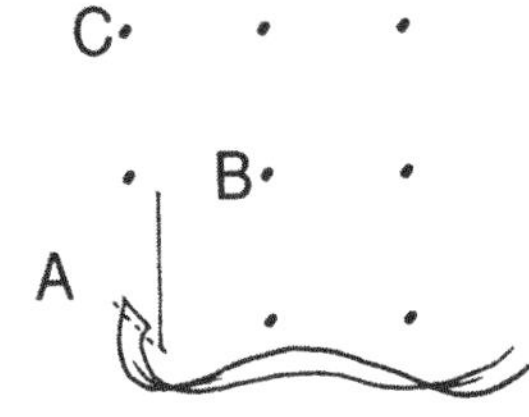

3 Stitch to dot B. Fold the ribbon over the cut end, and carry it to dot B. Stitch it in place.

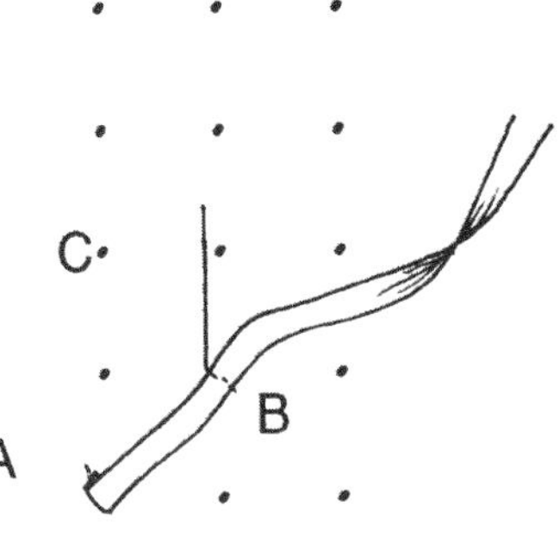

4 Stitch to dot C. Fold the ribbon over accordion-style, and carry it to dot C. Stitch it in place. Continue in the same manner until you reach the top dot.

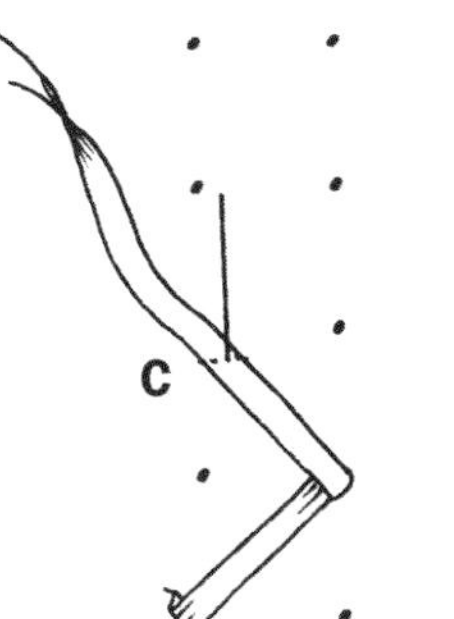

5 At the top, carry the ribbon straight across to the first dot in the next row, and anchor it in place. Work your way down the second row, crisscrossing your previously stitched ribbon as you go.

Picket Fence

Every storybook garden needs a picket fence. Use 7mm ribbon for a large design or 4mm ribbon for a smaller area.

1 Draw slashed lines for the top and bottom of the fence with an air-soluble marker Lay the two horizontal fence rails with flat ribbon running the full length of the fence between the slashed lines. Anchor each horizontal ribbon at the beginning and end.

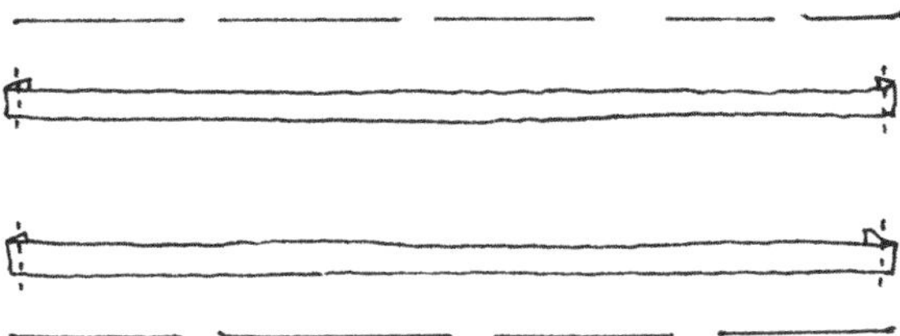

2 Beginning at the marker line at the fence bottom, lay ribbon perpendicular to the horizontal rails and anchor it at the base. Stitch beside the ribbon to the top fence rail. Fold ribbon as shown. Continue sewing through all thicknesses to the top line.

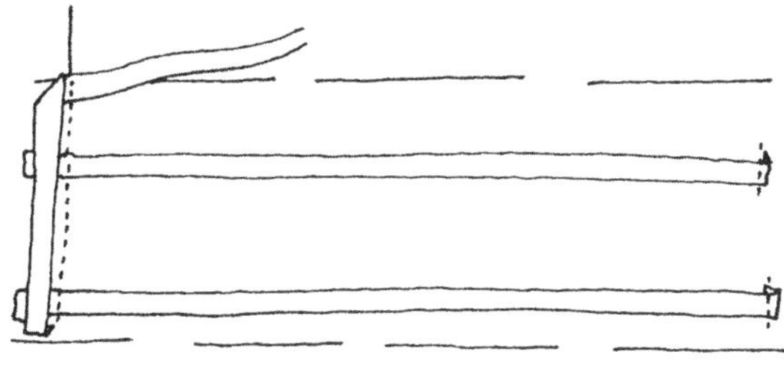

3 Fold the ribbon as shown to make your first picket.

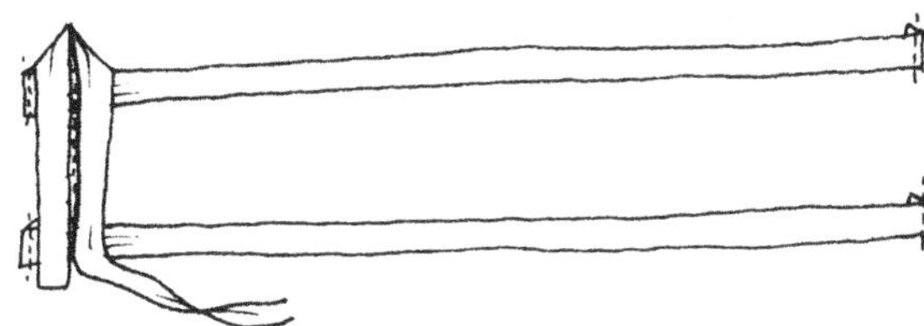

4 Stitch back down the center of the vertical pickets, tacking them with couching stitches where they cross the rails. Lay your next picket in place, folding and stitching the ribbon the opposite way on the bottom. Stitch it in place, as shown.

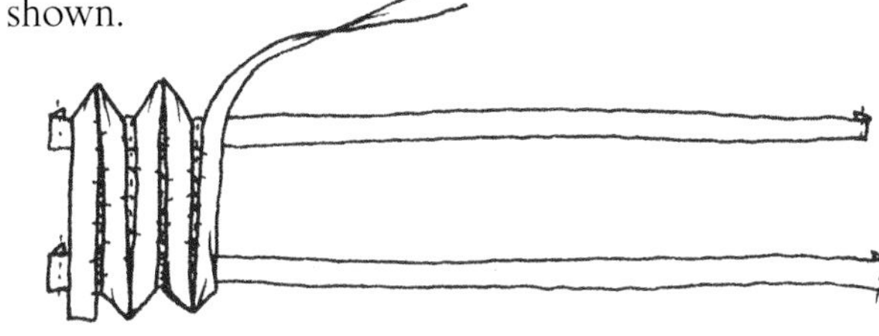

5 Continue working across the fence.

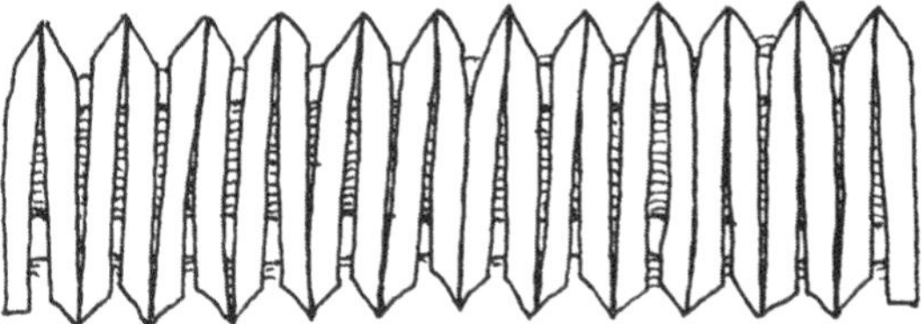

Hint: Keep perspective in mind when you create a fence. You may want some flowers or bushes behind the fence, and more flowers in front. Anything that will be behind the fence must be stitched before you make the fence. After stitching the fence, you can embellish the area in front with a garden of flowers.

An up-close look at the bunny jumper shows the garden fence and flowers in detail.

Fern-Stitch Basket

Use fern stitches to create a lush flower basket of 2mm or 4mm ribbon. When adding flowers and leaves, stitch a few that fall over the edges of the basket. For realism, weave some stems behind the basket handle by pulling the ribbon under the handle with tweezers as you work.

1 Draw a basket outline with an air-soluble marker. Divide the basket into vertical sections $3/8$" to $1/2$" wide, as shown.

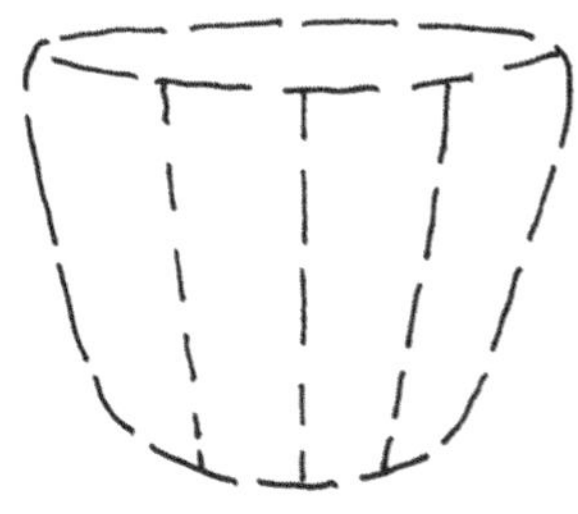

2 Work fern stitches from the bottom up to the top of one section.

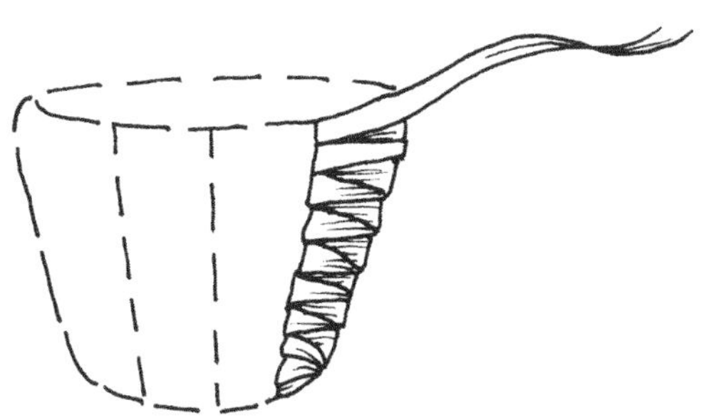

3 Carry the ribbon to the top of the adjacent section and stitch your way back down to the bottom of the basket, continuing until you've filled all basket sections.

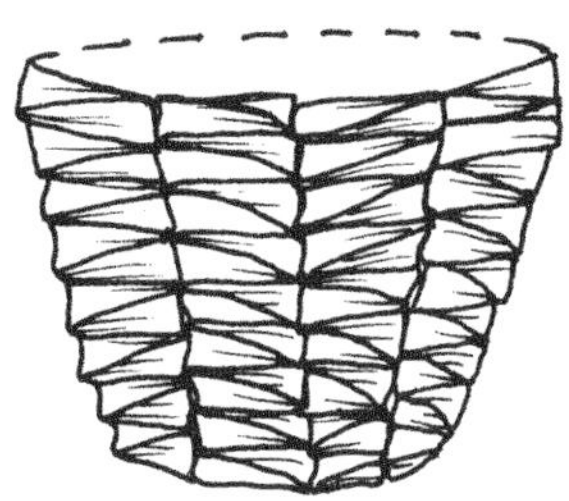

4 Stitch contrasting chain stitches along the edges of each section and at the top and bottom for details. Use chain stitches for a lightweight basket handle, and lazy daisy chain stitches for a heavier handle.

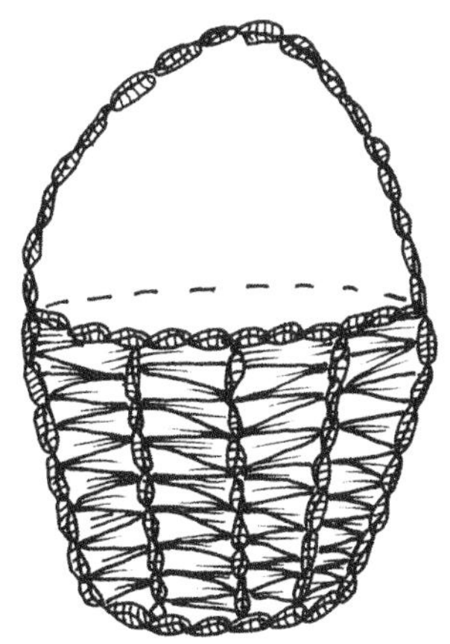

Woven Basket

A woven ribbon basket makes a lovely flower container. Try 2mm or 4mm ribbon for this basket. You also can use this type of ribbon weaving for making a window box, filling in hats, and so forth.

1 Draw a basket outline with an air-soluble marker. Lay a ribbon at the basket-corner bottom with the cut end toward the center. Tack the ribbon on the line, as shown.

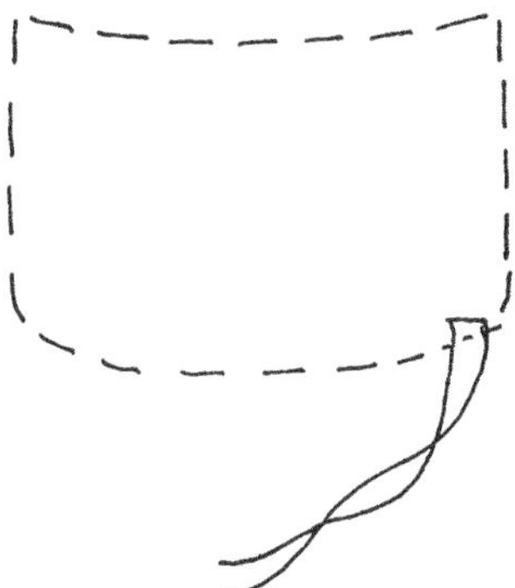

2 Stitch to the top of the basket.

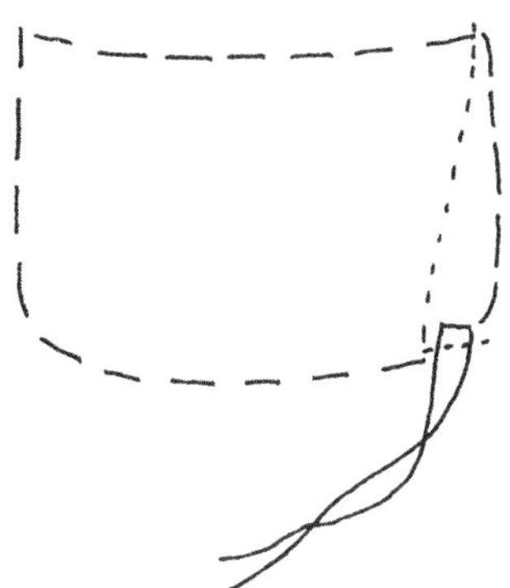

3 Carry the ribbon to the top, keeping it flat, and stitch to anchor it in place. Continue carrying and stitching the ribbon at the bottom and top across the entire basket to cover the drawn shape, ending at the bottom. Do not cut the ribbon.

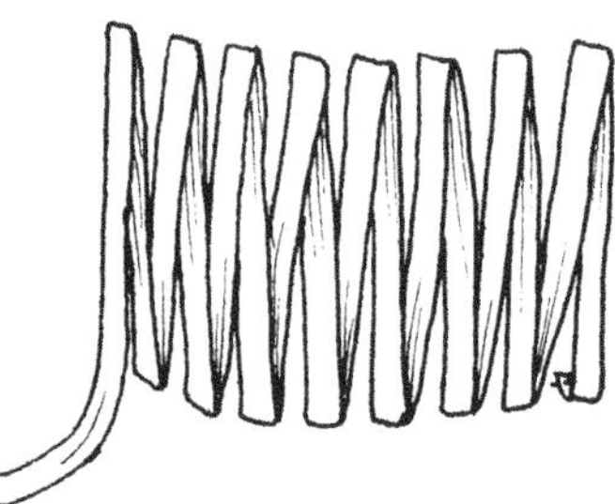

4 Using your tweezers, weave the ribbon over and under from left to right. When you get to the right side, tack the ribbon, making certain that it lies flat. Don't pull the ribbon too tight. Weave it to the left side and tack it in place.

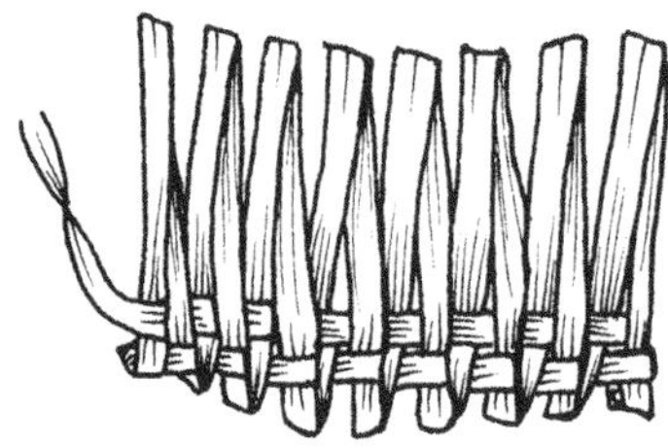

5 Weave the ribbon over and under and back and forth until the entire basket is filled.

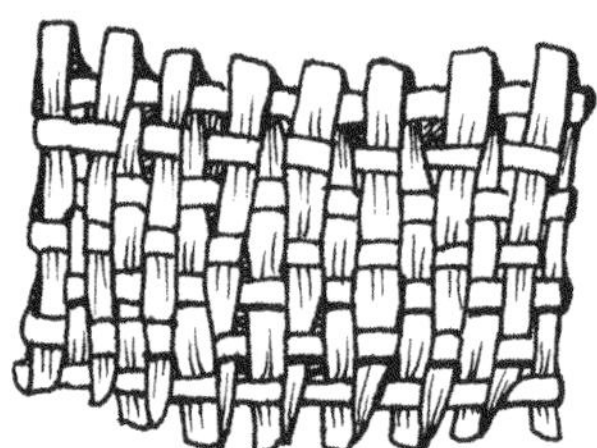

Hint: If your basket has rounded corners, you may have to start the ribbon over several times where it doesn't extend all the way to the bottom or the side edge.

Add a chain-stitch handle if you like, and fill the basket with your favorite flowers. Be sure to let some flowers and leaves fall over the edges of the basket. To make your basket appear more realistic, stitch some flower stems in front of the handle and some behind it. Pull the working ribbons for the flowers, leaves, and stems behind the handle with tweezers as you work.

Chain-Stitch Basket

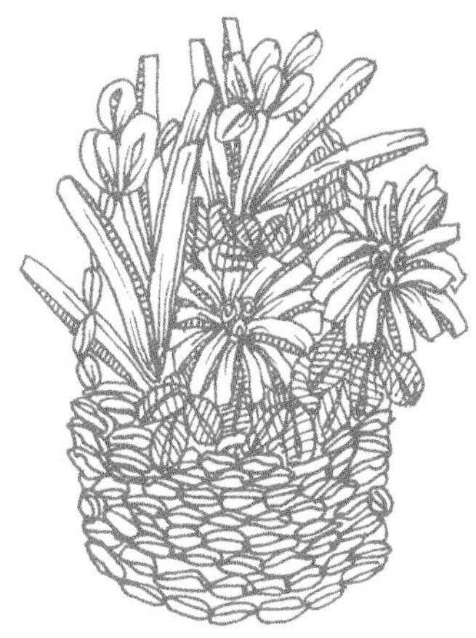

You can use chain stitches to make a variety of basket shapes. Use 2mm or 4mm ribbon or textured ribbon, heavy thread, or boucle yarn to add dimension.

1 Draw a basket outline with an air-soluble marker.

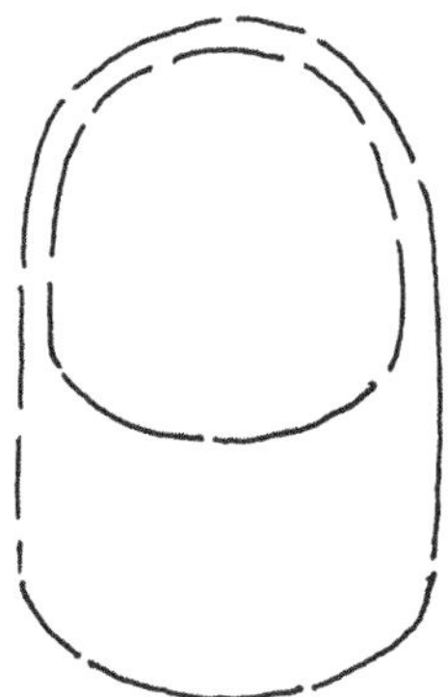

2 Work chain stitches across the bottom of the basket, make a U-turn at the side, and work back across.

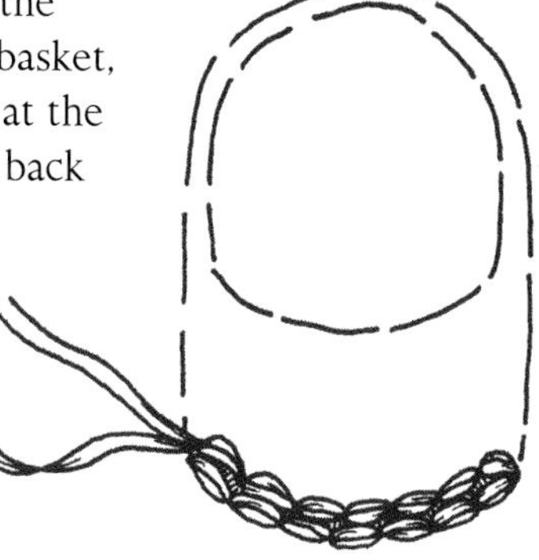

3 Fill the entire basket shape with horizontal rows of chain stitches. Work a chain-stitch handle.

Basket Shapes

Here are some basket shapes you can trace. These shapes are suitable for any of the techniques we've shown. The more unusual shapes are easiest to work in chain stitches; the squarer shapes would be more suitable for weaving.

Hint: Many photocopiers have enlargement and reduction options. Enlarge or reduce these shapes until the design is the size you need.

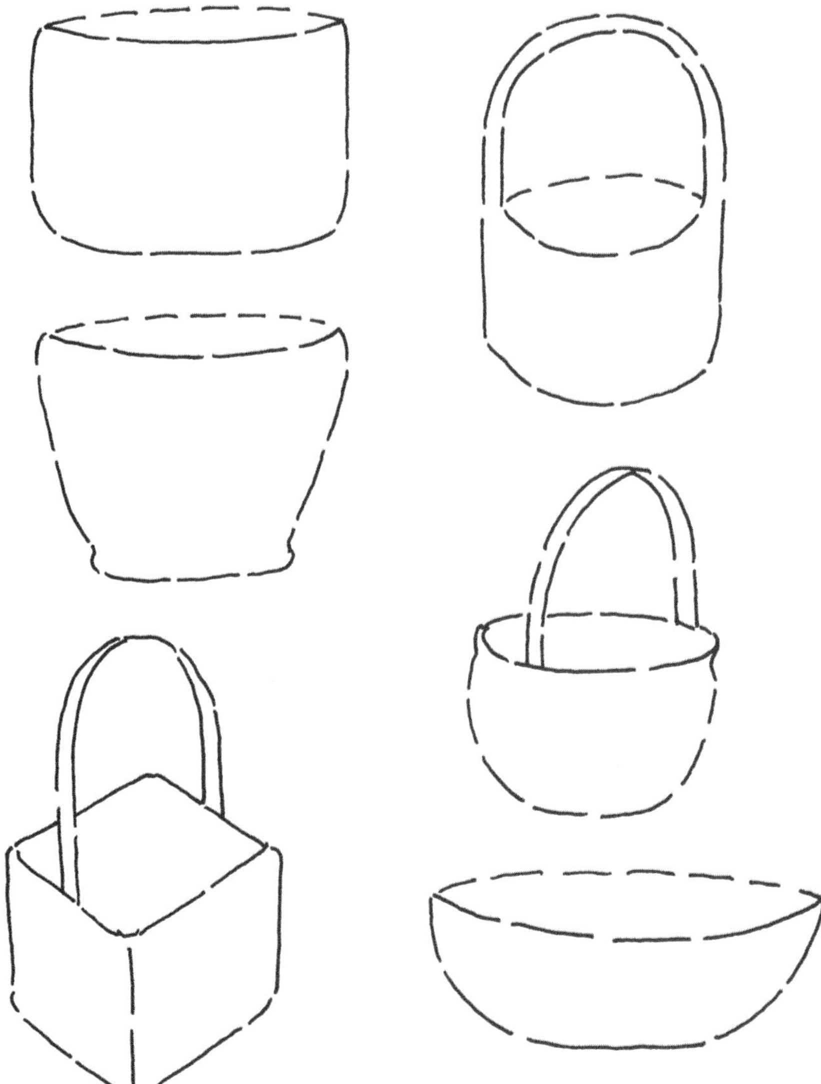

Flowerpots

Stitch flowerpots much like baskets. Choose 4mm ribbon for a smooth, rounded-edge chain-stitched pot, 4mm or 7mm ribbon for a fern-stitched square pot, or 7mm couched ribbon for any square pot shape.

1. Draw a flowerpot outline with an air-soluble marker.

2. Work chain stitches across the bottom of the pot saucer and the pot rim. Work chain stitches up and down the body of the pot for a smooth-textured flowerpot.

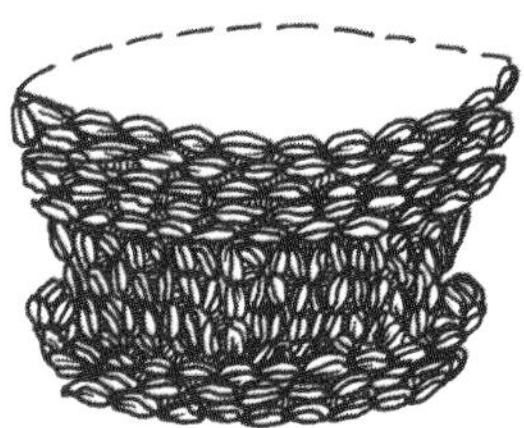

3. Or, work fern stitches across the face of a square flowerpot.

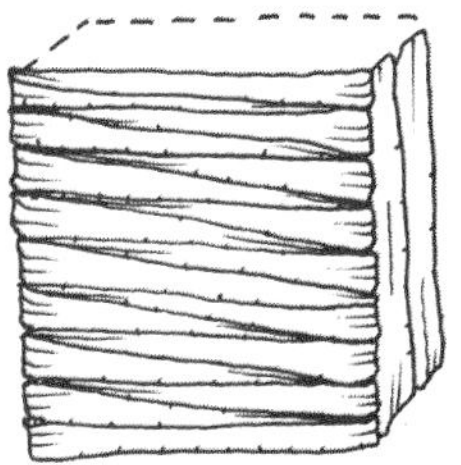

Flowerpot Shapes

Pot shapes vary from the traditional to the avant-garde. Create your own shapes—here are some you can trace to get started. Enlarge or reduce the shapes as needed for your project.

CHAPTER SIX

Garden Visitors

Flowers and bugs just naturally go together. Bees help to pollinate flowers and use the pollen to make honey. One of the joys of summer is seeing butterflies and dragonflies gliding around flower gardens and enjoying their beautiful colors. Here's how to create these insects in colors to match or contrast with your project.

Display your machine ribbon embroidery on purchased garments. Here, garden critters adorn a variety of wearables.

Bumblebee

Use 2mm light-yellow and 4mm bright-yellow ribbons and black pearl rayon to create lifelike bumblebees. Some of the details we'll show you are difficult to work on the machine. If you've also done some hand stitching, you may prefer to add these details by hand.

1. Work two light-yellow lazy daisy stitches at a 45-degree angle to make bee wings, as shown. Cut the ribbon, tuck it under a stitch, and tack it in place.

2. Work a larger bright-yellow lazy daisy stitch at the midpoint of the stitches you just made to make the bee body. Cut the ribbon, tuck it under a stitch, and tack it in place.

3. Anchor black pearl rayon near the bottom of the body. Stitch across 1/8", carry the pearl rayon across body, and anchor it.

4. Working with tweezers, pull the pearl rayon under the yellow body to the midsection. Stitch to the midpoint of the body, and pinch the yellow ribbon to form a waist. Anchor the

black thread there and stitch across the body, carrying the black thread; anchor it in place. This makes the second stripe across the bee body. Repeat to make a third stripe above the second.

5 Pull the pearl rayon behind the body to the top, and make a French knot for the head.

HAND-STITCHED DETAIL VARIATION

1 Follow steps 1 and 2 to make the wings and body.

2 Thread a large hand sewing needle with black pearl rayon, and make a small knot at the end. Bring the thread up from the back side of the fabric at the tail end, and make one stitch over the body from side to side (the entire stitch will be a scant 1/8").

3 Carry the thread on the wrong side of the fabric to the midpoint of the bee body. Bring the thread up to stitch a band across the midsection. Pinch the ribbon slightly to give the bee a waist. Carry the thread on the wrong side and work another stitch a scant 1/8" above the first waist stitch.

4 Carry the thread on the wrong side of the fabric to the bee head, and work a French knot to cover the tip of the ribbon and form the bee's head (wrap the thread around the needle three or four times). Take the thread to the wrong side of the fabric and make a couple of stitches (invisible from the right side) to anchor the thread end.

Ladybug

Stitch ladybugs wherever you want to add a touch of realism. You can stitch the ladybug's spots by machine or by hand. Make your ladybugs from 4mm red ribbon and black pearl rayon.

1 Work a red lazy daisy stitch about 3/8" long. Make certain that the sides of the stitch are loose enough to lie nearly flat. Cut the ribbon, tuck the end under, and tack it in place.

2 To make an antenna, work a lazy daisy stitch in black pearl rayon thread at a slight angle to the ribbon lazy daisy stitch; make a second stitch at about a 45-degree angle to the first to make the other antenna. This step can be stitched by hand or by machine.

3 Work a French knot for the head at the base of the antennae. Work two French-knot spots on each wing atop the red ribbon. These French knots must be small, so wrap one twist around the needle only. Cut the pearl rayon between each knot. Apply a seam sealant so the knot and threads won't fray.

Ants

What picnic or garden would be complete without a hill of ants? Use 4mm black ribbon for stitching ants, and add details of black pearl rayon by machine or by hand.

1 Work a 1/4"- to 1/2"-long horizontal ribbon lazy daisy stitch.

2 Work two bent antennae in black pearl rayon by making lazy daisy stitches with an extra stitch in the middle. Start a lazy daisy stitch as usual, but at the halfway point, tack and "bend," then complete the tip. Tack and bend the lazy daisy stitch on the return also. Carry the black thread against the ribbon body to the point where you'll start the next antenna, and repeat.

3 To make three sets of legs, repeat the antennae, stitching evenly along each side of the body and couching one stitch across the midpoint of the body. Make sure that this couching stitch gathers the ribbon slightly to form the sections of the ant's body.

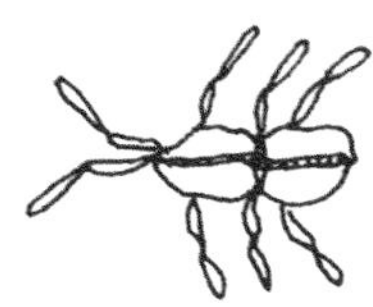

Spiders

Garden spiders are wonderful creatures, especially when you weave a mysterious web of thread for them. Use 4mm black ribbon to make the arachnoid.

1 Work a 3/8" lazy daisy stitch. Do not cut the ribbon.

2 Work a French knot for the spider's head. Cut the ribbon, tuck the end under the stitch, and tack it in place.

3 Work two black pearl rayon antennae by making two lazy daisy stitches. Carry the thread next to the spider's head from one antenna to the other.

4 Work four bent legs in black pearl rayon on each side of the body by making lazy daisy stitches with an extra stitch in the middle. Start a lazy daisy stitch as usual, but at the halfway point, tack and bend it. Then complete the tip. Tack and bend the lazy daisy stitch on the return, too. Carry the black thread against the body to the point where you'll start the next leg. Continue in this manner to make eight legs for a daddy-longlegs spider. Or, make a short-legged spider with regular lazy daisy legs.

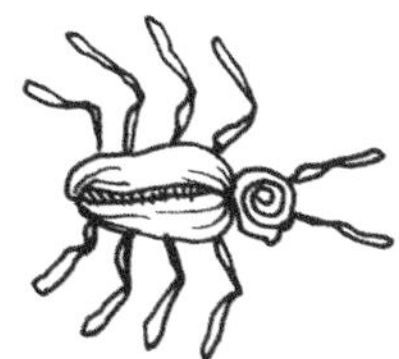

Spiderweb

Make your spiderwebs before you work your flowers. Then, as you complete the flowers, you can make some of them overlap the webs. Try a variety of threads for your webs. Gray pearl rayon and gray woolly nylon make especially realistic webs.

1 Draw a web with an air-soluble marker or trace the one shown here.

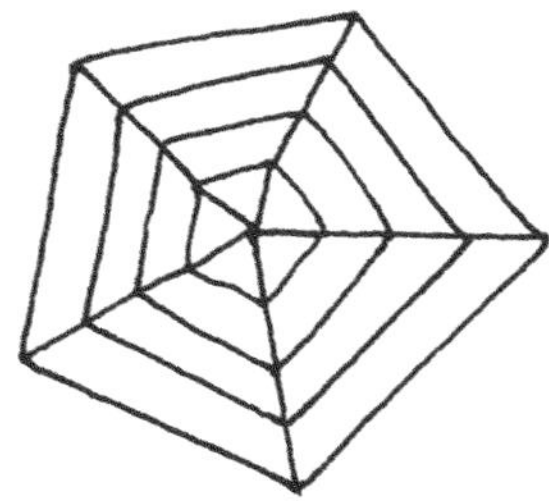

2 Work a web of thread, couching as you go. Follow the web outline from the center to the outer edges.

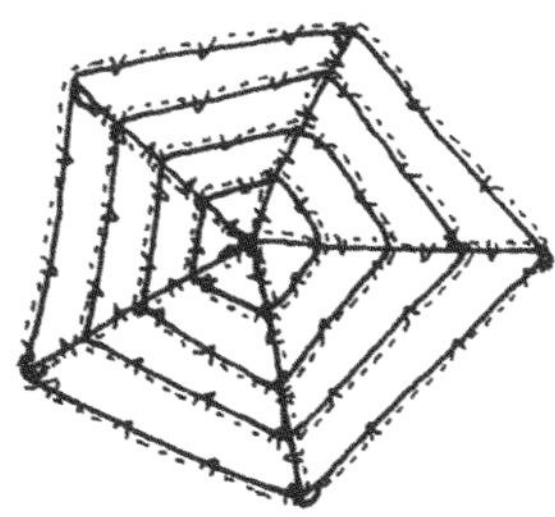

Butterflies

You can make a variety of beautiful butterflies with just a few well-placed lazy daisy stitches. Use 4mm gold, black, and plum ribbons for the bodies, heads, and upper wings and 7mm purple ribbon for lower wings and black pearl rayon thread for antennae.

1 Work a gold ribbon lazy daisy chain of two stitches for the butterfly body. Do not cut the ribbon.

2 Work a French knot for the head at one end of the lazy daisy chain. Cut the ribbon, tuck the end under, and tack it in place.

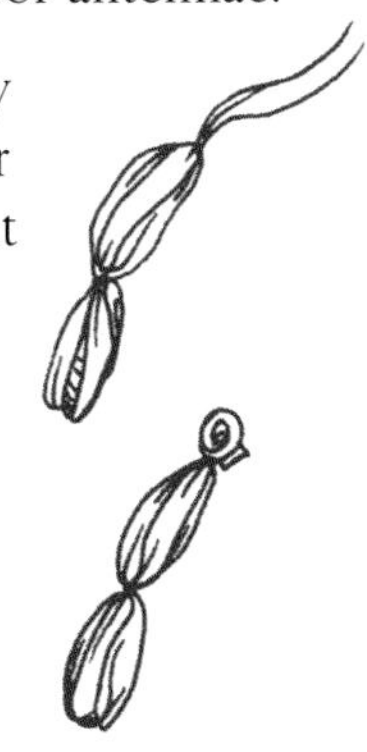

3 Work two sets of three lazy daisy stitches with black ribbon angling down slightly on each

side of the butterfly body. Carry the ribbon from one side to the other under the body by pulling it through with your tweezers.

4 Work two sets of three elongated lazy daisy stitches with purple ribbon above the black stitches, angling them up slightly. Make the purple stitches longer than the black stitches.

5 Work two sets of three small lazy daisy stitches with plum ribbon on top of the elongated purple stitches.

6 Work a French knot with black pearl rayon thread about 3/8" above the butterfly head.

7 Stitch back to the head, carrying the pearl rayon, and tack it to the head. Carry the pearl rayon out from the head about 1/8" from the first French knot. Tack the thread and work a French knot at the end.

Make a profile of a butterfly by adding a slight curve to the body and omitting one set of wings.

Hummingbird

Birds are attracted to flowers, and they make a lifelike addition to any garden scene. Make our birds in any color combination that enhances the flowers in your garden. Use 7mm ribbon for the bodies; 4mm ribbon for the tails, heads, and wings (in two shades); and black pearl rayon for the bills and eyes.

1 Work one long ribbon stitch with 7mm ribbon for the body. Start at the head, and pinch the ribbon while you anchor it. Stitch toward the tail about 1" and tack the end.

2 Work tail feathers with 4mm ribbon. Anchor the ribbon at the outer ends of the top tail feathers. Stitch the ribbon to the body, holding it out of the way. Anchor it and stitch away from the body for a second tail feather, anchoring the second feather at an angle.

3 Work three flat lazy daisy stitches for the next tail feathers. Angle the stitches so they spread at the back of the bird's body.

4 Work six or seven flat lazy daisy stitches for the wing that radiates upward from the opposite side of the body.

5 Work a flat lazy daisy stitch across the flat end of the lazy daisy stitches with a contrasting color of ribbon. To make your bird look as through it's fluttering its wings, add a second flat lazy daisy stitch at a 45-degree angle to the first one.

6 For the head, use two different colors of 4mm ribbon to work two short ribbon stitches. Work the stitches close together or let them overlap slightly.

7 Work a flat lazy daisy stitch of black pearl rayon for the bill. Work a French knot of black pearl rayon for the eye near the top of the head.

This crazy-quilt teddy bear is elegant enough to take to high tea. Use the techniques in Chapter 7 for sewing and embellishing the patches. Then, stitch him together using a commercial pattern.

CHAPTER SEVEN

Crazy Quilting

As children, we slept under heavy wool crazy quilts that had been stitched together by our foremothers from scraps. The pieces were embellished with seam-line stitching in a variety of styles; some of it looked like flowers and some like chicken tracks. These stitches, slowly done by hand, added interest and personality to these warm quilts. You can duplicate these embellishments—not only for quilts, but also for vests, Christmas socks, tree skirts, placemats, toys, and table runners. Here this century-old technique is updated with fast and easy crazy quilting and stitches.

CRAZY-QUILT CONSTRUCTION

Crazy quilting by machine is fast and fun, and it's an ideal way to use up favorite bits and pieces from your fabric stash. Begin by sorting out a variety of fabrics. If you plan to embellish the fabrics with ribbon embroidery, you'll want to choose solid colors and muted prints so the fabric doesn't overwhelm your stitching. Most firmly woven fabrics are suitable for crazy quilting—from velvets and satins to denims and linens. Just keep the end use in mind, and be sure all of the fabrics are washable if you plan to launder the garment.

Hint: You'll find it easier to clean your completed crazy-quilted projects if you use scraps that have the same care requirements. Mixing silks and denims may look good, but when cleaning is necessary, you'll have to clean the entire piece by the method required for the most delicate fabric used.

Use a base or foundation fabric for your crazy quilt. This base fabric is never seen in the finished piece. The base fabric should be lightweight like muslin or cotton broadcloth. Here we use a Christmas-stocking to illustrate the basic directions for crazy quilting.

1 Choose several pieces of fabric, each large enough to fit in your hoop. Sew some of your favorite flowers in the center of each piece. Your motifs can be as simple as a single small violet or as elaborate as a garland of roses, depending on the scale of your finished project. A larger

project even can accommodate a garland as its focal point, surrounded by smaller areas of embroidery. Likewise, a small stocking or ornament requires a smaller flower or critter.

2 Trim the embellished fabric for the focal point to a five-sided irregular shape, leaving at least 1" around the embroidery on all sides.

3 Set your sewing machine to sew with a straight stitch. Pin the focal-point fabric in the center of the base fabric. Stitch the fabric in place around all sides about 1/8" in from the edges.

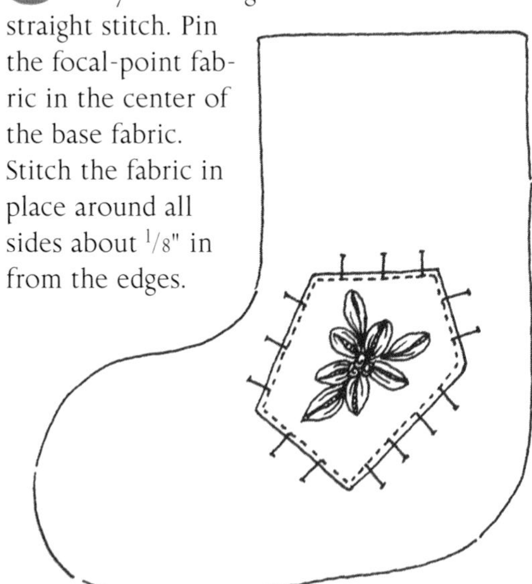

4 Select a fabric scrap of a contrasting color, and place it right side down on top of the embroidered piece, aligning the edges as shown. Stitch through all layers along the aligned edges, using a 1/4" seam allowance.

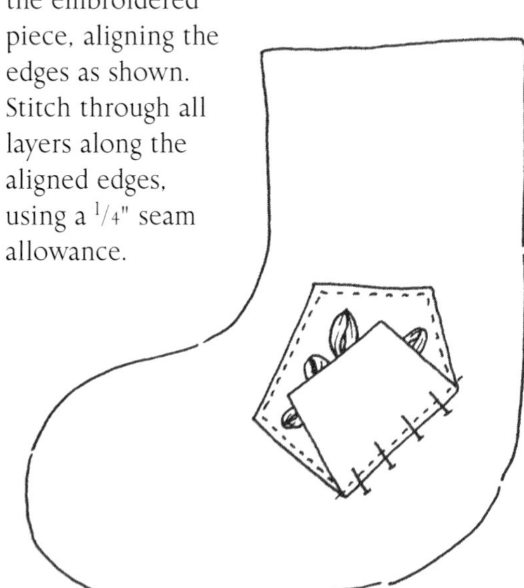

5 Open up the plain piece so the right side faces up. Finger-press the seam (run your fingernail along the seam so it lies flat). If necessary, pin the fabric to lie flat. Trim the edges even with the embroidered piece.

This easy-to-sew holiday stocking and ornament are made of crazy-quilt pieced-and-stitched satin fabric scraps. Work the patchwork and embellishment first, then cut out and sew your favorite ornament and stocking shapes.

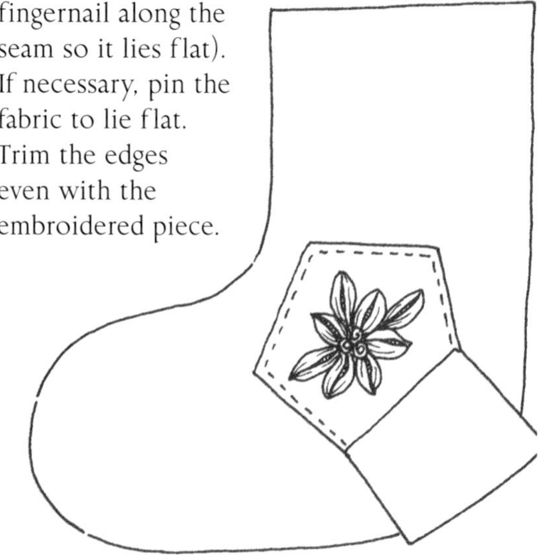

6 Add other fabric pieces around your focal-point piece in the same manner using both plain and embroidered fabrics. Don't worry if some raw edges show—you'll cover them with stitching or trim later.

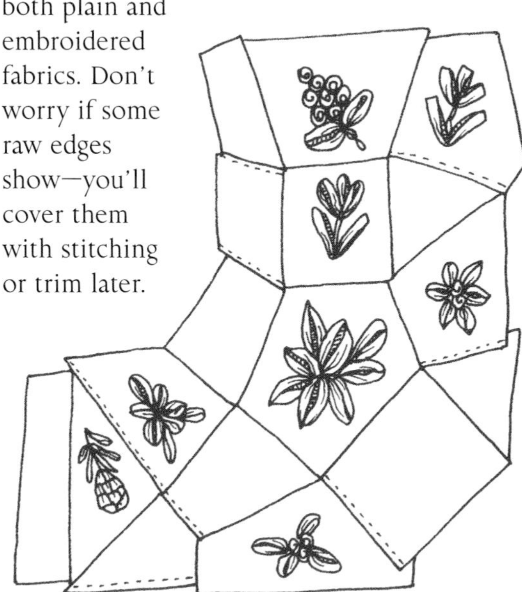

7 When the base fabric is covered, you'll conceal the raw edges in one of several ways:

- Select stitches from the pages that follow, and cover the raw edges with embroidered ribbon stitches.
- Use machine decorative stitches to cover the raw edges.
- Cover the raw edges with narrow trims, laces, and fancy ribbons.
- Use a combination of these three techniques.

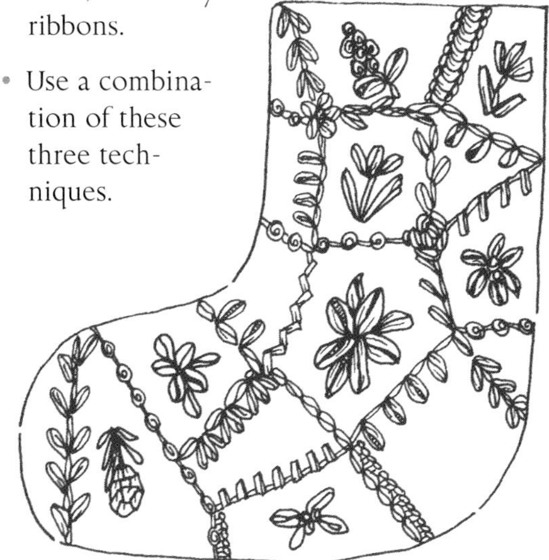

CRAZY-QUILT STITCHES

Crazy-quilt stitches traditionally are used to cover patchwork seams. But you also can use them as border stitches on any of your work. Make your stitching as simple as a couched line of ribbon or as complex as a row of roses—it's all part of the fun of crazy quilting.

Feather Stitch

Use 2mm or 4mm ribbon for this traditional crazy-quilt stitch.

1 Draw a line of dots 1/4" apart with an air-soluble marker.

2 Anchor the ribbon at the first dot and stitch to the second dot.

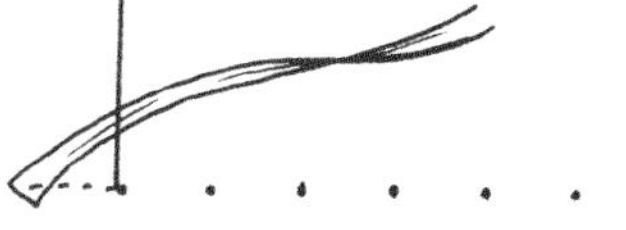

3 Carry the ribbon to the second dot, and anchor it with a couple of stitches. Work a lazy daisy stitch at a 45-degree angle.

4 Work a lazy daisy stitch at a 45-degree angle below the one you just made.

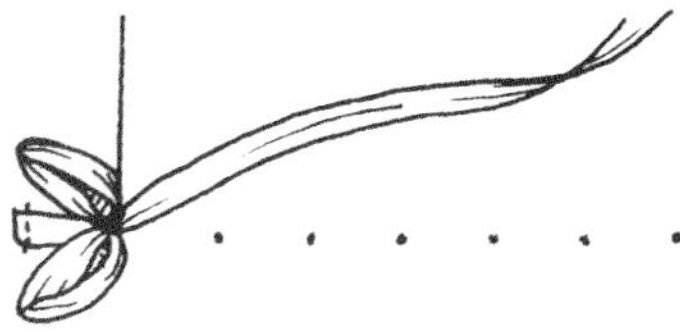

5 Continue working in this manner until the row of stitching is complete and the seam is covered.

3 Make a second flat lazy daisy stitch perpendicular to the second dot. Continue working in this manner until the row of stitching is complete and the seam is covered.

Half Feather Stitch

Work the half feather stitch as you do the regular feather stitch with 2mm or 4mm ribbon, but make only one lazy daisy stitch each time, alternating sides. You can get different looks by keeping the ribbon flat or scrunching it.

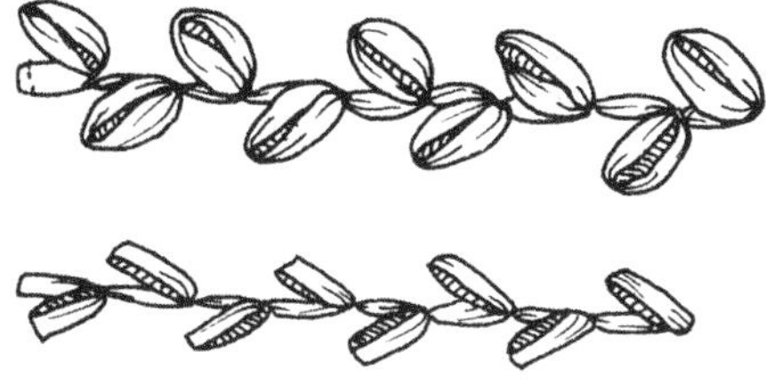

Blanket Stitch

This perennial favorite works well for covering a seam or accenting a folded edge. Use 2mm or 4mm ribbon for best results.

1 Draw a line of dots 1/4" apart with an air-soluble marker. Anchor the end of the ribbon at the first dot. Work a flat lazy daisy stitch perpendicular to the first dot. Keep the ribbon flat, and fold it over on itself accordion-style.

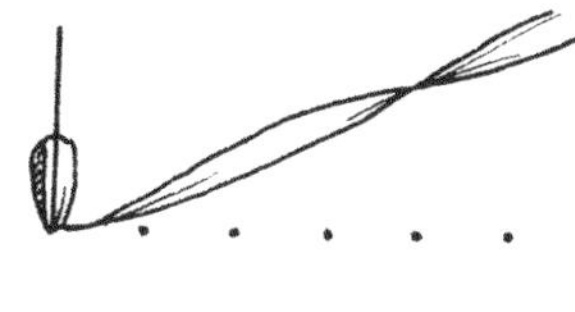

2 Stitch to the next dot and then carry the ribbon, keeping it flat. Stitch to anchor the ribbon.

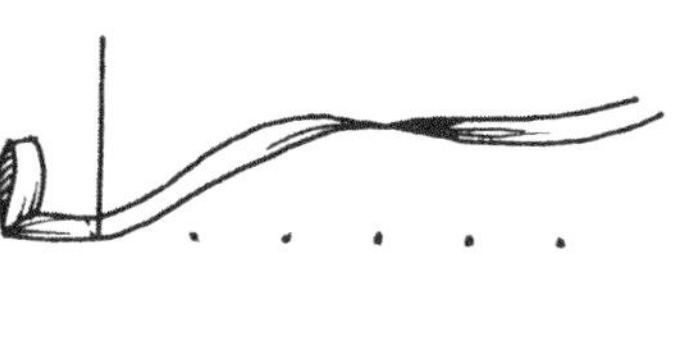

Zigzag Stitch

Use 2mm or 4mm ribbon for this tidy-looking stitch.

1 Draw two lines of staggered dots 1/2" apart with an air-soluble marker. Anchor the end of the ribbon at the first dot in row one.

2 Stitch out at a 45-degree angle between the first dot in row one and the first dot in row two. Carry the ribbon to the first dot in row two, keeping it flat, and anchor it.

3 Stitch to the second dot in the first row. Fold the ribbon accordion-style, keeping it flat. Bring the ribbon to the second dot in the first row and anchor it. Continue working in this manner until the row of stitching is complete and the seam is covered.

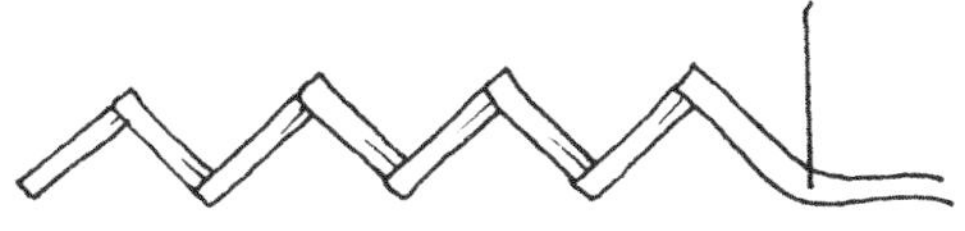

Cross-Stitch

Make cross-stitches just like lattice stitches, but on a smaller scale. Use 2mm or 4mm ribbon to work the stitches.

1 Draw two lines of staggered dots 1/2" apart with an air-soluble marker. Anchor the end of the ribbon at the first dot and work a line of zigzag stitches. When you reach the end of the line, use an air-soluble marker to draw a dot between each of the completed zigzags.

2 Work a second row of zigzag stitches over new dots using a matching or contrasting color of ribbon.

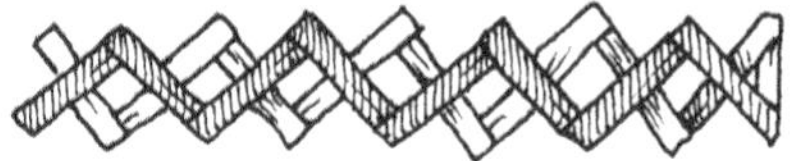

Pistil Stitch

This seed-bearing part of a flower works up well in 2mm ribbon or pearl rayon thread.

1 Draw a line of dots 1/2" to 3/4" apart with an air-soluble marker. Anchor the end of the ribbon at the first dot.

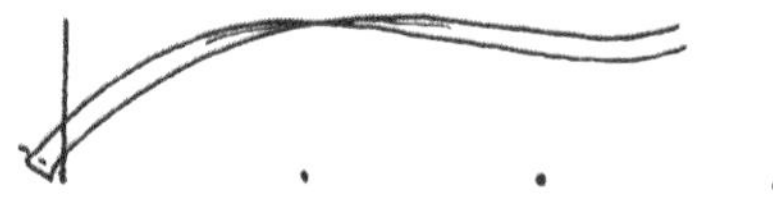

2 Stitch straight up from the first dot 1/4" to 1/2", carry the ribbon flat, and anchor it.

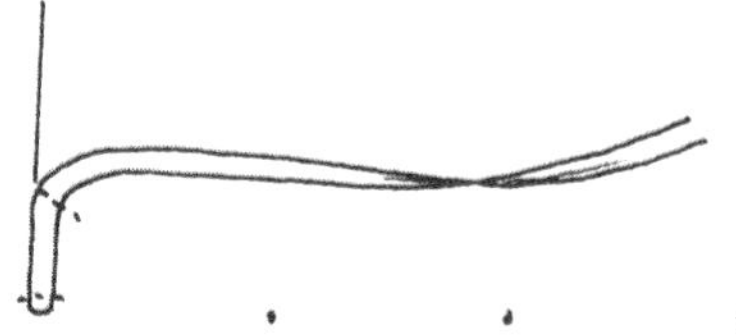

3 Work a French knot at the anchor. Stitch back to the first dot, carry the ribbon flat, and anchor it.

4 Repeat steps 2 and 3 twice, making one stitch at a 45-degree angle on each side of the first stitch.

5 Stitch to the next dot, carry the ribbon, and repeat steps 1 through 4 for another set of pistil stitches. Continue working in this manner until the row of stitching is complete and the seam is covered.

Double Lazy Daisy Chain

Make a luxurious lazy daisy chain with two colors of 2mm or 4mm ribbon.

1 Work a lazy daisy stitch with two colors of the same-width ribbon.

2 Stitch through the middle of the lazy daisy stitch to the outer point.

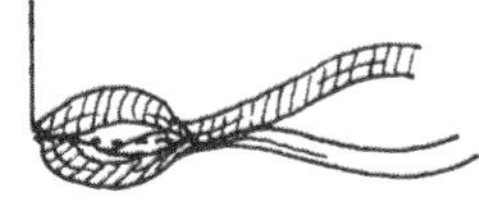

3 Carry the ribbons to the opposite end of stitch, keeping them flat, and anchor them.

4 Continue working in this manner until the row of stitching is complete and the seam is covered.

French-Knot Chain

Use 2mm or 4mm ribbon to make this dainty chain of stitches.

1 Draw a line of dots 3/8" apart with an air-soluble marker. Anchor the end of the ribbon at the first dot, and work a French knot.

2 Stitch to the next dot, carry the ribbon, and anchor it.

3 Work a French knot. Then continue in this manner until the row of stitching is complete and the seam is covered.

Crazy-quilt stitches add pizzazz to a classic tuxedo shirt. Stitch lines of crazy-quilt ribbon embroidery atop selected pleats. Outline the bib and collar stand with fancier stitches.

Couching

Couch a pretty ribbon or trim to creatively conceal raw edges or seams. Use metallic ribbons or textured yarns in widths to complement the scale of your project.

Couching with a Twist

Ordinary ribbons take on new dimension when you put a twist in the ribbon between each tacking point.

Lazy Daisy Clusters

Work a row of lazy daisy stitches to enliven your crazy-quilt garden. Choose 2mm, 4mm, or 7mm ribbon for this row of flowers.

1. Draw a line of dots 1/2" apart with an air-soluble marker. Anchor the end of the ribbon at the first dot and work a vertical lazy daisy stitch.

2. Work two more lazy daisy stitches, one on each side of the first one you worked. Start the bottom of each stitch at the same dot.

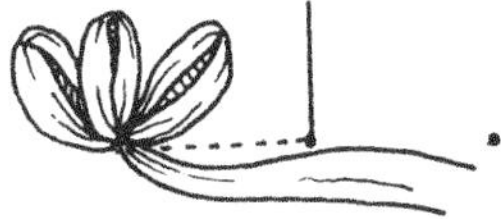

3. Carry the ribbon, anchor it at the next dot, and continue working clusters of lazy daisy stitches in the same manner until the row of stitching is complete and the seam is covered.

CRAZY-QUILT STITCH COMBINATIONS

There are endless possibilities for combining ribbon embroidery stitches for crazy quilting. Here are a few of our favorites.

Bullion Roses with Lazy Daisy Stitches

Use 7mm ribbon for the roses and 4mm or 7mm green ribbon for the lazy daisy leaves.

1. Draw a line of dots 1/2" apart with an air-soluble marker. Anchor the end of the ribbon for the bullion rose at the first dot and work the first rose. Cut the ribbon, stitch to the second dot, and make the next rose. Continue working in this manner until the row of roses is complete.

2. Anchor the end of the leaf ribbon at the first rose and work one lazy daisy stitch, covering the cut end of the ribbon. Stitch to the next rose.

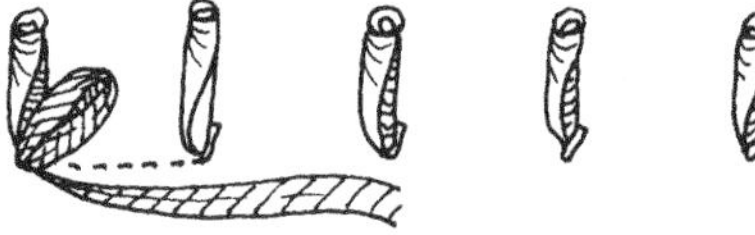

3. Carry the ribbon and work a lazy daisy stitch at the base of the second rose. Continue working lazy daisy stitches at the base of each rose until the row is complete.

Embellished Lazy Daisy Stitch

Work rows of these special lazy daisy flowers with 4mm ribbon for both blooms and leaves.

1. Draw a line of dots 1/2" apart with an air-soluble marker. Anchor the end of the ribbon for the flowers at the first dot and

work three lazy daisy stitches. Cut the ribbon between the flowers, stitch to the next dot, and make three more lazy daisy stitches. Continue working in this manner until the row of daisies is complete.

2 Anchor the end of the green ribbon at the first dot. Work a lazy-daisy-stitch leaf on each side of the flower. Stitch to the next flower.

3 Carry the ribbon and anchor it at the second dot. Make two more lazy-daisy-stitch leaves. Continue working in this manner until the row of lazy daisy leaves is complete.

Blanket Stitch with Zigzag

Work this variation of the blanket stitch with two colors of 4mm ribbon. Use tweezers to weave the ribbons in and out of the stitches.

1 Work a row of blanket stitches all the way across the seam with the first color of ribbon. Anchor and cut the ribbon. Anchor the end of the second color of ribbon 1/2" above the first blanket stitch.

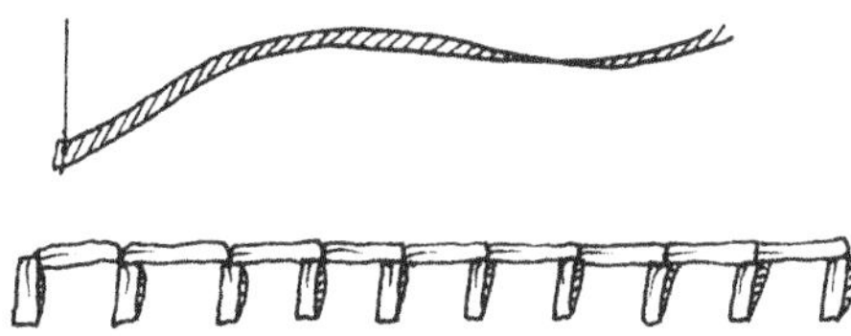

2 Stitch down to the second blanket stitch. Carry the ribbon and weave it under the blanket stitch. Bring the ribbon up on the opposite side of the blanket stitch. Stitch to a point 1/2" above the third blanket stitch and anchor the ribbon.

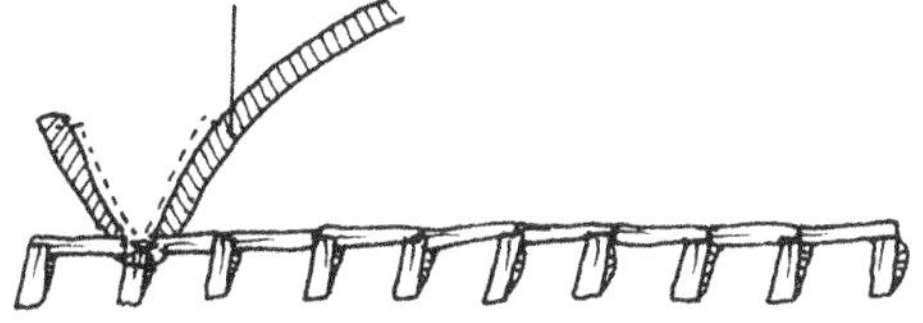

3 Continue weaving contrasting ribbon in and out of the blanket stitches in this manner until the row of stitching is complete and the seam is covered.

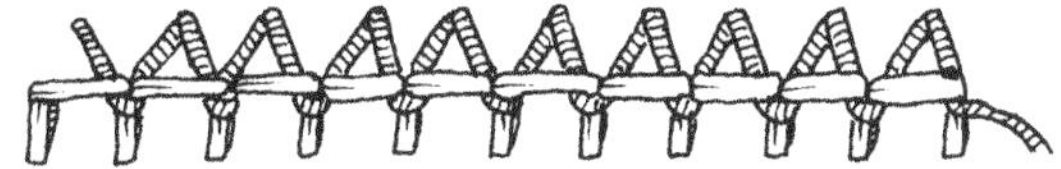

CHAPTER EIGHT

Monograms and More

Some of the first things a young child learns to read are the letters that start his or her first and last names. Our initials and their combinations are important, but they also can be works of art and decorations. Take your first or last initial—or combine all three of your initials for a monogram—then enhance the design and enjoy the compliments you receive.

Embellished Block Initial

This bold and beautiful style of letter first is filled in with fern stitches and then embellished with leaves and flowers. Choose 4mm ribbon for the block letter, 2mm or 4mm ribbon for the letter outlines and flower stems, and 7mm ribbon for the leaves and flowers.

1. Draw selected initials with an air-soluble marker.

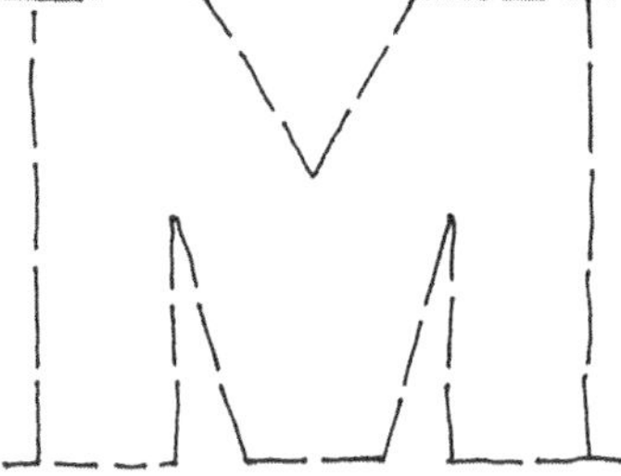

2. Work fern stitches using 4mm ribbon to fill in the entire initial.

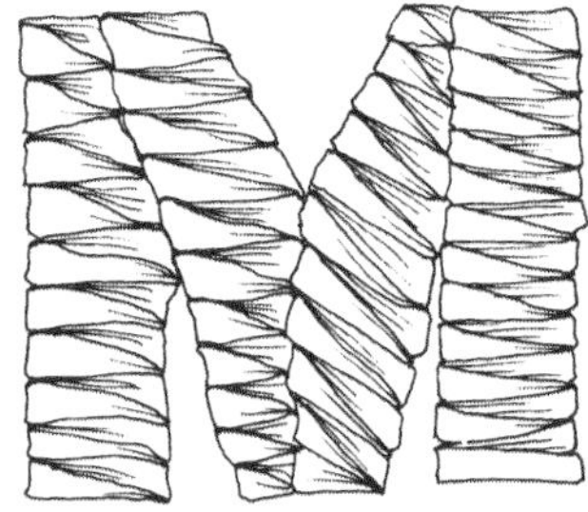

3. Work a chain-stitch outline using a contrasting shade of 2mm or 4mm ribbon.

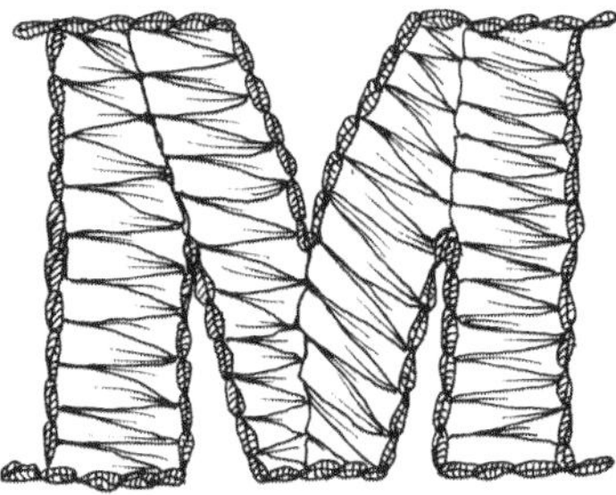

4. Work chain-stitch stems using 2mm or 4mm ribbon. To make the stems weave in and out, work chain stitches up to the edge of the letter and remove the hoop from the sewing machine. Thread both ends of the ribbon onto a tapestry hand needle, and pull the

A delicate initial with carefully selected flowers embellishes this silk blouse.

Embroidering an initial, a carefree dragonfly, and a few decorative flowers onto a denim shirt is a good way to practice. The shirt is quick to stitch and fun to wear.

ribbons to the back side of the fabric. Carry the ribbons across the back and come out at the opposite edge of the letter. Replace the hoop under the machine needle and continue to work chain-stitch stems.

5 Work selected flowers and stems using 7mm ribbon.

Embellished Script Initial

Make this delicate-looking letter with 4mm or 7mm ribbon in twisted couched stitches or chain stitches. If you like, add flowers and leaves stitched with 4mm and 7mm ribbons.

1 Draw the selected initial with an air-soluble marker. Anchor the end of 4mm or 7mm ribbon at the beginning of the letter. Stitch 1/2", twist the ribbon one-half turn, and anchor it with a few stitches.

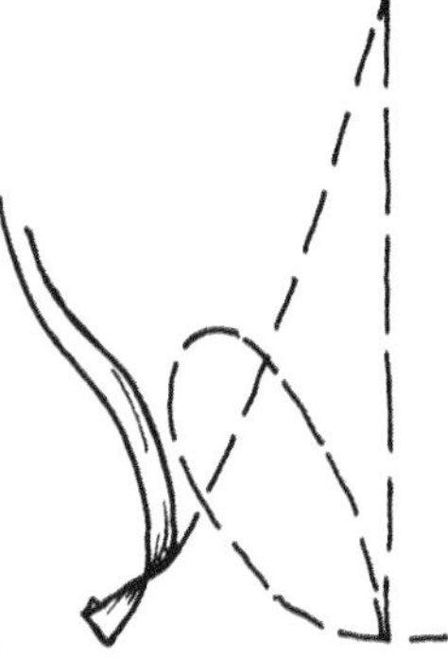

2 Continue twisting the ribbon and stitching it in place until the letter is completely covered.

3 Or, work chain stitches around the letter until it is completely covered.

4 Work selected flowers and stems using 4mm and 7mm ribbons.

Alphabets

We've included two alphabets for your use. Trace the selected pattern and draw it on your fabric with an air-soluble marker. You might want to use your own handwriting for your design. Use a photocopier if you need to enlarge or reduce your letters to fit a particular space.

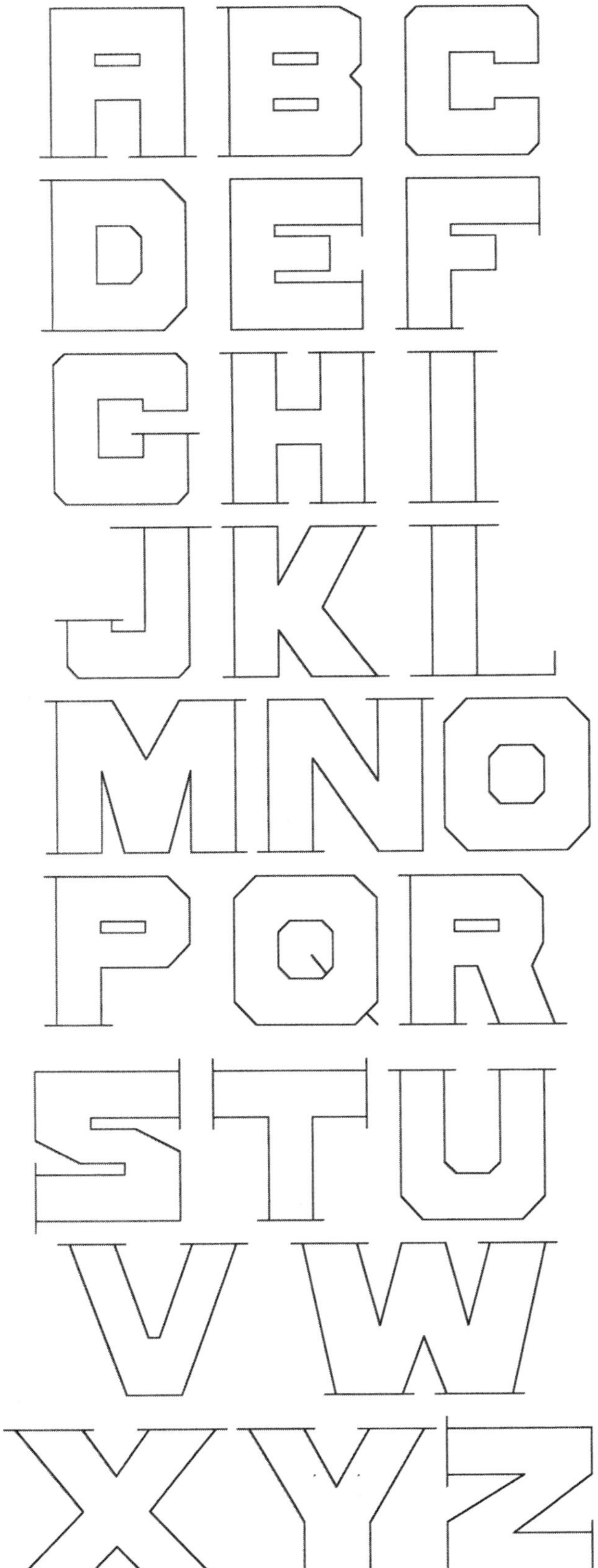

CHAPTER NINE

Projects

Now that you have mastered the basic stitches, here are some projects to put your stitching skills to work. Before you know it, beautiful flowers and designs will be blooming on jackets, vests, pillows, book covers, and more!

Amy's Window Pocket

In the wee hours of the night, our friend Amy Opalk dreamed of a lace-curtained window with a window box full of geraniums and other flowers. In the morning, she stitched her dream on a fabric scrap and appliquéd it to a shirt pocket. Amy chose a brick-pattern fabric for her pocket background.

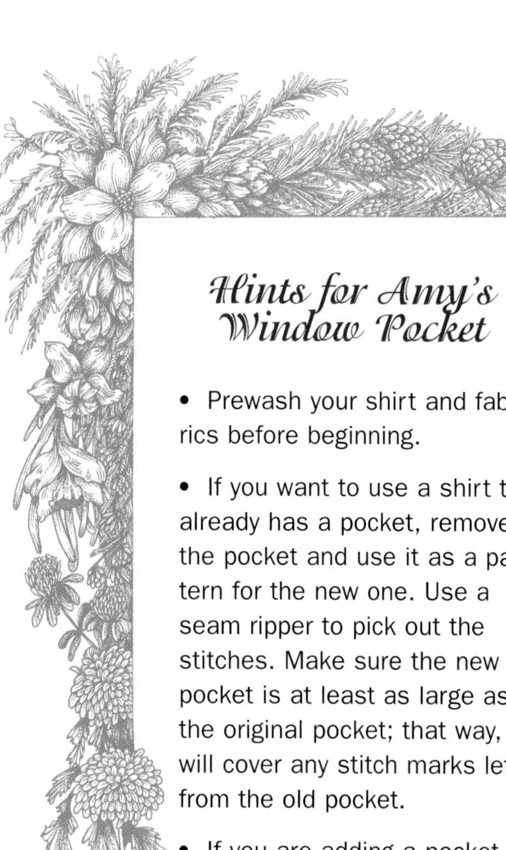

Hints for Amy's Window Pocket

- Prewash your shirt and fabrics before beginning.
- If you want to use a shirt that already has a pocket, remove the pocket and use it as a pattern for the new one. Use a seam ripper to pick out the stitches. Make sure the new pocket is at least as large as the original pocket; that way, it will cover any stitch marks left from the old pocket.
- If you are adding a pocket to a shirt that never had one, be sure to check the size and location of your pocket by trying on the shirt first. Fold the background fabric to the approximate size of your finished pocket, pin it on your shirt, and then try the shirt on to make sure the location is flattering (by decorating the pocket, you automatically draw attention to it). Mark the location with an air–soluble marker or chalk, and continue with step 1.
- Don't limit Amy's Window to pockets! It's a fun decoration to add to pillows, vests, jean jackets, or any other item you'd like to enhance with charming embellishment.

Materials

Purchased shirt
8" x 8" square of fabric for background
3" x 3" square of dark fabric for window background
4" x 6" piece of lace scrap for curtains
Ribbons: 4mm light green, medium green, bright green, yellow green, avocado green, yellow, lavender, and red
Bouclé yarn or curly thread for window box
Tear-away fabric stabilizer
Air-soluble marker

DIRECTIONS

1. Draw a pocket shape on the background fabric with an air-soluble marker.

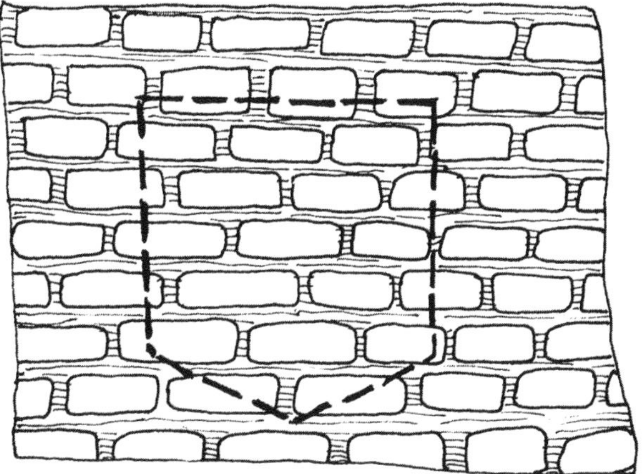

2. Cut the window background to size and pin it to the background fabric. With sewing machine set for regular sewing, straight-stitch around all edges of the window background.

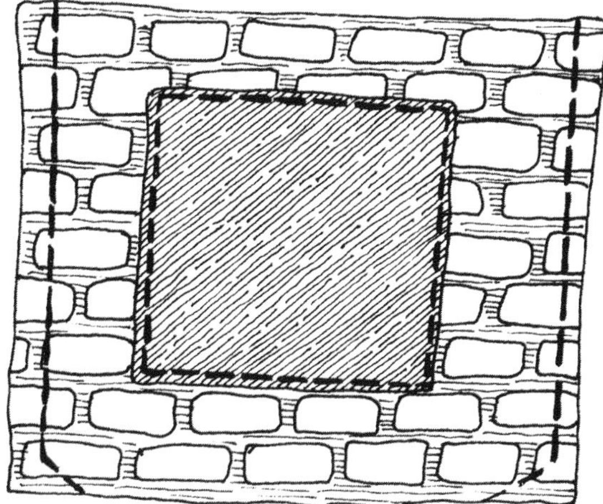

3 Cut the lace to the same height as the window opening but slightly wider. Baste the lace in place, gathering it slightly at the top and bottom.

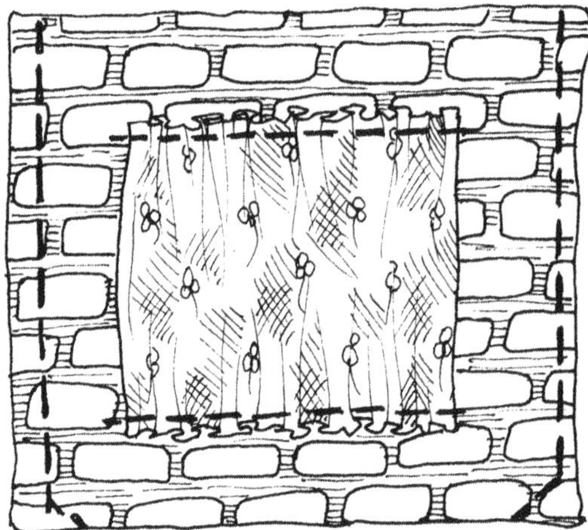

4 Set your sewing machine for a satin stitch by doing the following:

- Use an appliqué or satin-stitch foot.
- Set the machine for a wide zigzag stitch, and "fine" or .05 stitch length.
- Engage the feed dogs.
- Loosen the upper thread tension by one number.

5 Place a piece of tear-away stabilizer under the pocket fabric. Satin-stitch the top and sides of the window, covering the raw edges of the lace. Satin-stitch straight lines for windowpanes. Tear away the fabric stabilizer.

6 Place the background fabric in a hoop and set your machine for ribbon embroidery. Work flowers over the bottom of the lace curtain. The window box will cover the flower-stem ends.

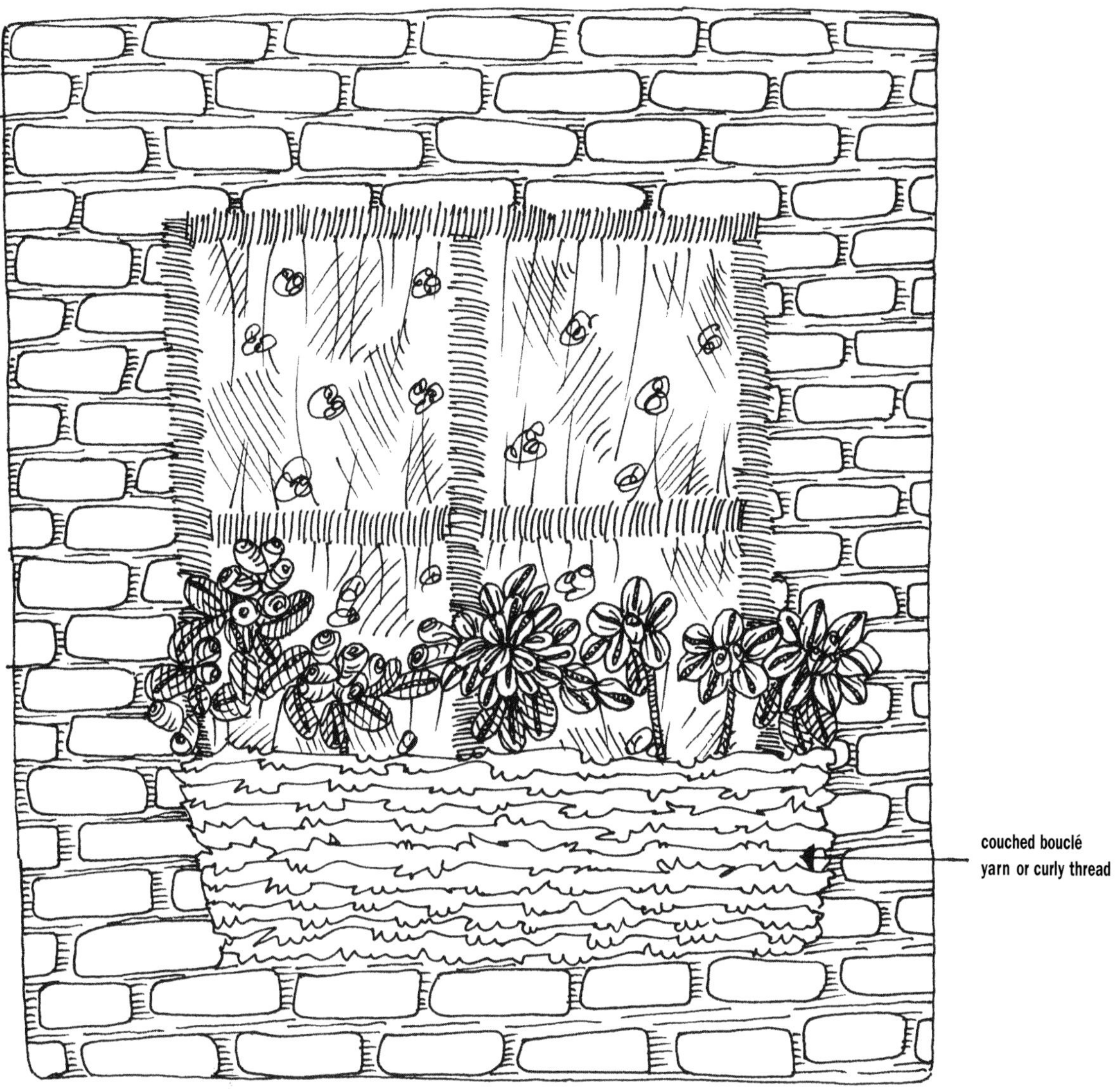

7 Work the window box with couched bouclé yarn or curly thread. If you prefer, you may weave the flower box or work the area in fern stitches.

8 Work flowers to fill any voids, allowing some petals to hang over the edges of the window box.

9 Trim the finished piece to pocket size plus a 1/2" seam allowance on sides and bottom. Allow 1" at the top. Hem the top edge of the pocket. Turn the cut edges under along the seam allowance and pin the piece to the shirt. Try on the shirt to check the alignment and placement. With your sewing machine set for regular sewing, straight-stitch or machine-blind-hem the piece to the shirt front.

CHRISTMAS POTPOURRI

Christmas is the time of year we all look forward to, as much for the decorations as the good cheer. Whether they're for home decorating or gift giving, these holiday projects will enhance your yuletide season.

Christmas-Tree Towel

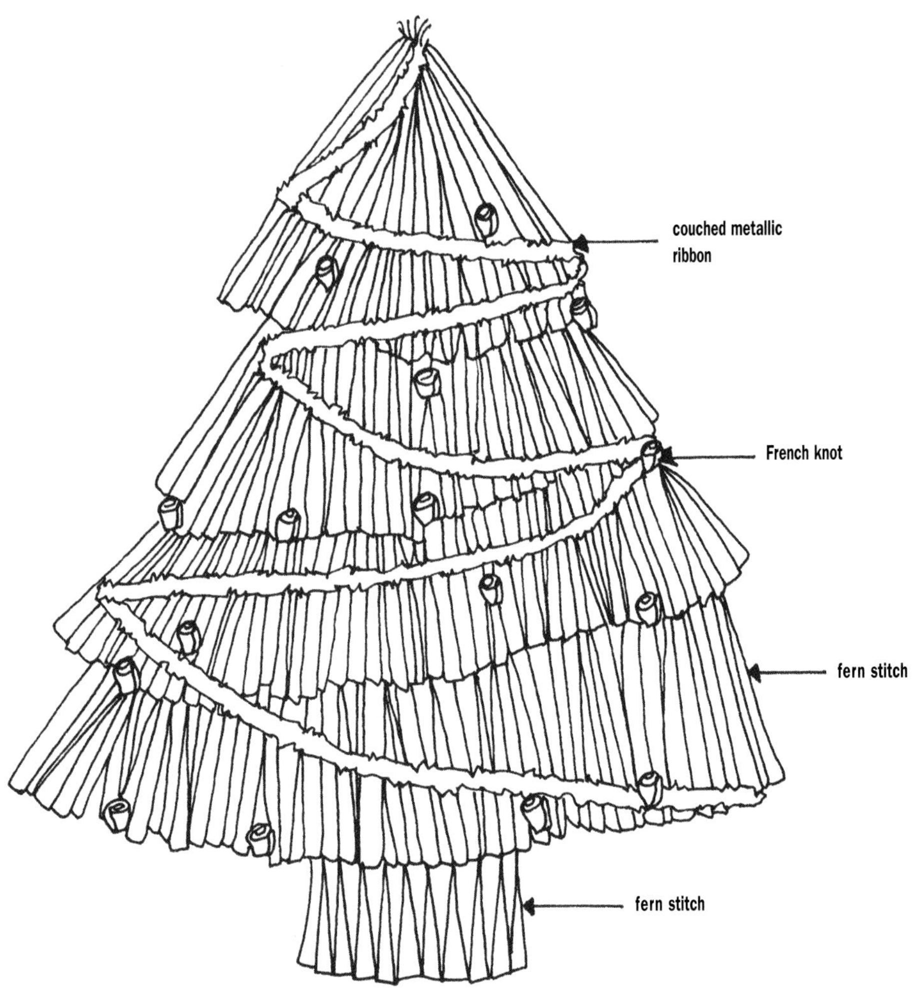

Materials

Purchased hand towel
Ribbons: 2mm green and red; 4mm white, medium green, dark green and brown
Gold metallic decorative ribbon
Air-soluble marker

DIRECTIONS

1 Draw a tree shape on towel with an air-soluble marker. Work a short tree trunk in fern stitches with brown ribbon. Keep the ribbon close together and the stitches dense.

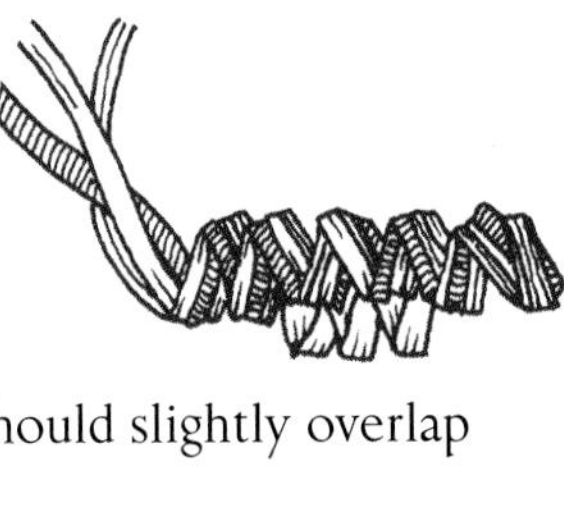

2 Work the bottom row of the tree in fern stitches with two or three shades of green ribbon used simultaneously. The bottom row should slightly overlap the top of the trunk.

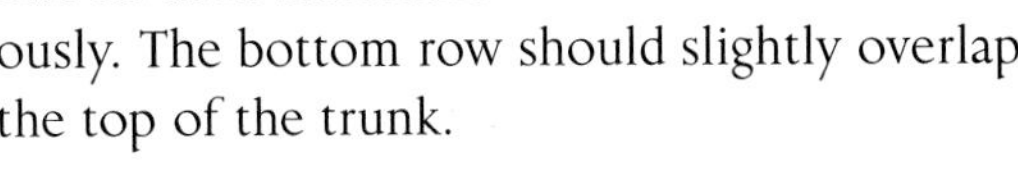

3 Carry the ribbon to the next row above and fill in the row.

Hint: To help fill in the area, lay your ribbons next to each other at the bottom and overlap them at the top.

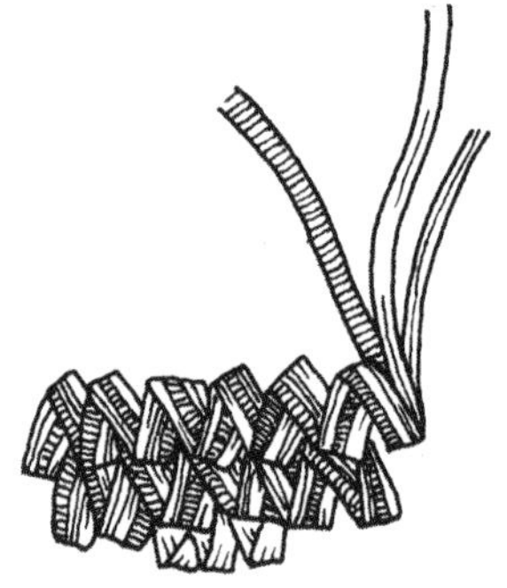

4 Work in this manner until you reach the top of the tree. Fold the ribbon ends under and tack them in place.

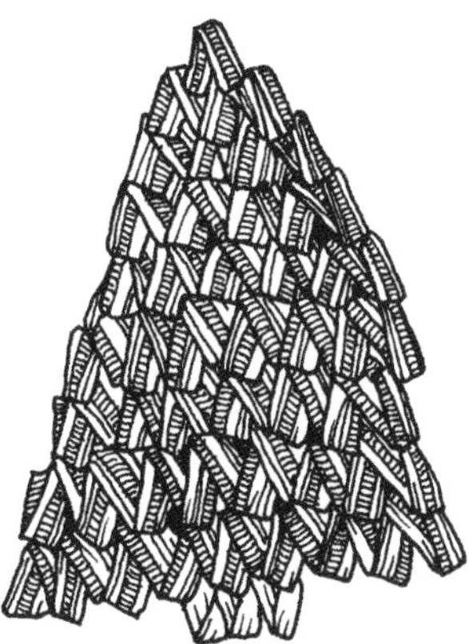

5 For ornaments, work bullion stitches or French knots with red and silver ribbons. Cut the ribbons between stitches. Work garlands of couched or chain-stitched metallic ribbon.

"Welcome" Door Decoration

Materials

Ribbons: 2mm red and dark green;
4mm in a variety of red shades;
7mm Christmas green
6" x 8" piece of white fabric
1 yard plaid bias piping for edging
⅓ yard plaid bias-covered cord for handle
6" x 8" piece of plaid fabric for backing
Polyester fiberfill
Hand sewing needle with large eye
Air-soluble marker

DIRECTIONS

1 Draw the outline of pillow and the word "Welcome" on white fabric with an air-soluble marker.

2 Work chain stitches in 2mm ribbon over all letters, beginning with the "W." At the end of the "W," cut the ribbon, tuck the end under the last stitch, and tack it in place.

3 Work chain stitches across the letters, beginning at the first "e" and ending at the beginning of the "c." Do not cut the ribbon.

4 Remove the hoop from the machine. Thread the ribbon ends on a hand sewing needle and pull to the back of the fabric. Bring the needle and the ribbons back to the top of the fabric at the top tail of the "c."

5 Replace the hoop under the machine needle and continue to work the chain-stitch "c." Stop again at the beginning of the "o." Repeat Step 3, coming up at the top of the "o," as shown.

6 Continue working the remaining letters. Cut the ribbon, tuck the ends under, and tack them in place.

7 Draw lines to represent the branches of a pine bough with an air-soluble marker. Work elongated lazy daisy stitches in various lengths with 2mm ribbon to cover the pine-bough and branch lines.

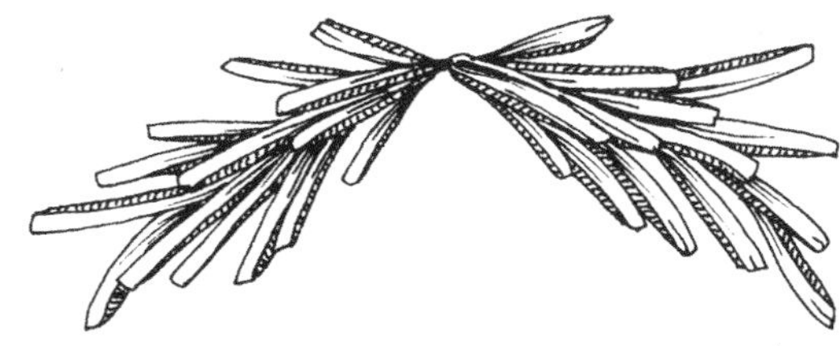

8 Draw holly leaves with an air-soluble marker.

9 Work loose ribbon stitches with 7mm ribbon to cover the shapes.

10 Stitch next to the ribbon and tack the points of the holly where they're drawn.

11 Work French knots or bullion knots with a variety of shades of red ribbons for the holly berries.

12 Work pinecones to fill in any gaps in the garland.

13 Work a row of feather stitches with 2mm green ribbon along pillow outline.

ASSEMBLY DIRECTIONS

1 Pin the bias piping in place on the right side of the embellished fabric. Pin covered cord in place for the handle. Baste.

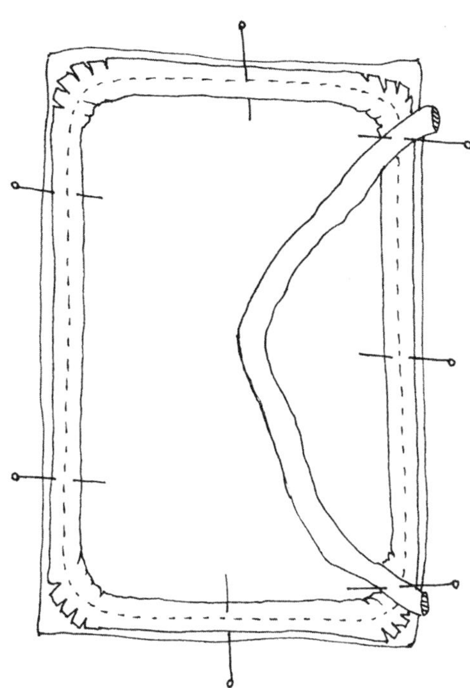

2 Cut the backing piece to match the front and lay the backing face down on the finished front. Pin the pieces together. With your sewing machine set for regular sewing, use a zipper or piping foot to sew next to the piping, leaving a 3½" opening along one side for turning and stuffing. Remove the pins, turn the piece to the right side.

3 Lightly stuff the piece with polyester fiberfill. Slip-stitch the opening closed.

Holiday Gift Bags

Materials

10" x 12" piece of off-white fabric
Ribbons: 2mm dark green; 4mm brown, red, and wine; 7mm green

DIRECTIONS

1 Near the center of the fabric, draw a 2½" x 8" rectangle (the outline of the bag) and the selected embellishments with an air-soluble marker.

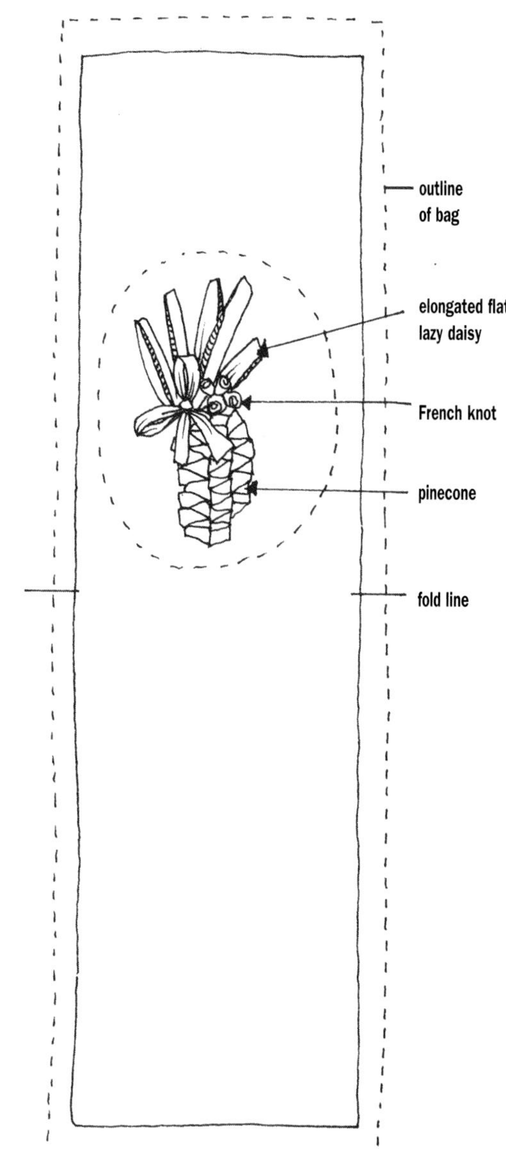

2 Work pinecones and pine branch with brown and green ribbons; work holly berries with red ribbon.

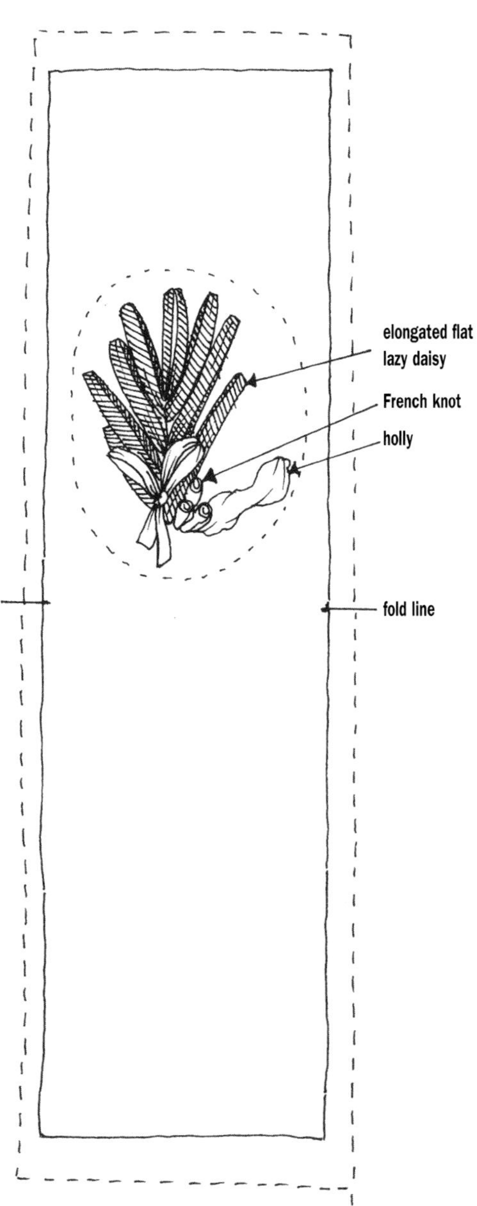

3 Trim the embellished fabric to size. Fold the fabric in half with the right sides together. With your sewing machine set up for regular sewing, stitch 1/4" side seams.

4 Turn the bag to the right side. Fray the top 3/4" edge of the bag. Stuff as desired and tie the bag closed with green ribbon.

Flower Sampler Pillow

A garden full of ribbon flowers decorates this pillow. Create the pillow top as you practice making flowers. Make your pillow a real sampler and use a different flower in each square. We'll introduce you to the three-stitch chain stitch, used here for stitching the long straight lines that divide the sampler.

Materials

18" x 18" square of muslin, linen, or Aida cloth for pillow top
Two 12" x 15" pieces of fabric for pillow back
2 yards of bias cording for pillow edge
Ribbons: 2mm yellow for pillow lines; assorted colors for flowers
Air-soluble marker
14" pillow form

DIRECTIONS

1 Draw a 14" square at the center of the fabric for the pillow top. Divide the square and draw lines for sixteen 3 1/2" squares.

2 Set your sewing machine for straight stitching and thread invisible thread through the needle and regular sewing thread in the bobbin. Change to an open-toe embroidery foot if you have one; otherwise, use the regular presser foot.

Place 36" of yellow ribbon atop the fabric. Take a few stitches through the ribbon at the center of its length to anchor it at the beginning of one of the lines. Carry the ribbon ends up between the toes of the presser foot and hold them out to the sides. Make three machine stitches forward through the fabric only and stop with the needle down.

3 Cross the ribbons in front of the needle. Make three more machine stitches, cross the ribbons in front of the needle. Continue in this manner until the first line is covered. Work all vertical lines in this manner. Then work all of the horizontal lines.

4 Work flowers to fill the squares as shown.

Fantasy Flower	Dandelion	Poppy	Violet
Iris	Single-edge Ruched Flower	Cascading Loop Flower	Calla Lily and Cattail
Geranium in Chain-Stitch Basket	Thistle	Judy's Mum	Loop-Stitch Flower in Fern-Stitch Basket
Lilac	Rose	Carnation	Sunflower

5 Trim the embellished pillow top to 15" square. Pin the bias piping in place on the right side. Baste.

6 Set your sewing machine for straight stitching. Turn one long edge of each pillow back piece to the wrong side 1/2" then again 1"; machine-stitch the hem in place.

7 With right sides together, pin the pillow back, overlapping, to the pillow top.

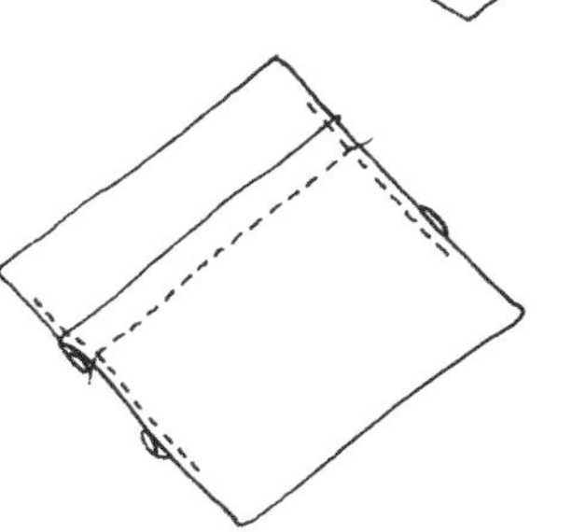

8 Stitch around the outside edges with a 1/2" seam allowance, using a zipper or piping foot. Turn to the right side and insert the pillow form.

Small Hatbox

This small velvet hatbox showcases fanciful ribbon flowers and is a stylish holder for jewelry and keepsakes. Cover a gift box with fabric if you can't find one ready-made that suits your color scheme.

Materials

9"x 9" square of white linen or Aida cloth
Ribbons: 4mm purple, pale green, medium green, and dark green; 7mm light avocado green, light peach, peach, and light blue
18" of purchased plum rattail cord
24" of purchased green braid
24" of purchased white braid
7½"–diameter, 4" high purchased fabric-covered miniature hatbox
Fabric glue
Air-soluble marker

DIRECTIONS

1. Draw flowers at the center of the white fabric with an air-soluble marker.
2. Work the flowers as shown.
3. Trim the embellished fabric to fit the box top and glue it in place with fabric glue.
4. Glue rattail and braids in place to cover the raw edges of the fabric. At a trim joint, tuck cut ends under while glue is wet.
5. Allow to dry overnight.

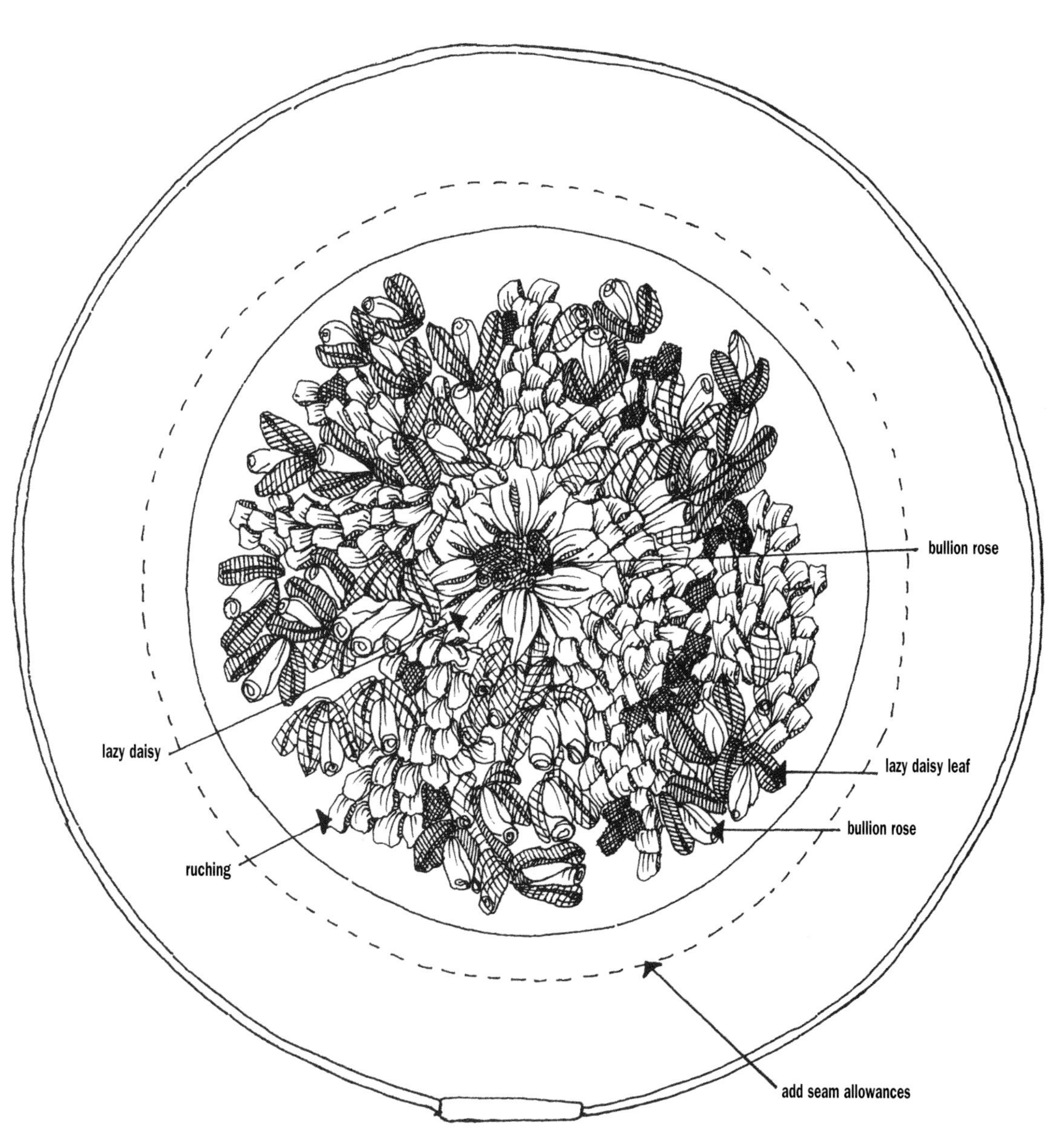

Embellished Wood Box

A colorful basket of ribbon posies gives this antique wooden cigar box a new lease on life. Look for boxes you can embellish the same way at craft stores and at tag sales.

Materials

9" x 9" square of white linen or Aida cloth
Ribbons: 2mm gold, grayed green, light avocado green; 4mm light gold, rose, pink, light peach, medium peach, cocoa brown, and plum; 7mm light avocado green and cream
24" of ½"-wide blue braid
7½" x 7" x 3" wooden cigar box

DIRECTIONS

1. Draw flowers at the center of the white fabric with an air-soluble marker.
2. Work the flowers as shown.
3. Trim the embellished fabric to fit the box top and affix it with fabric glue.
4. Glue trims in place to cover the raw edges of the fabric. At a trim joint, tuck the cut ends under while the glue is wet. Allow to dry overnight.

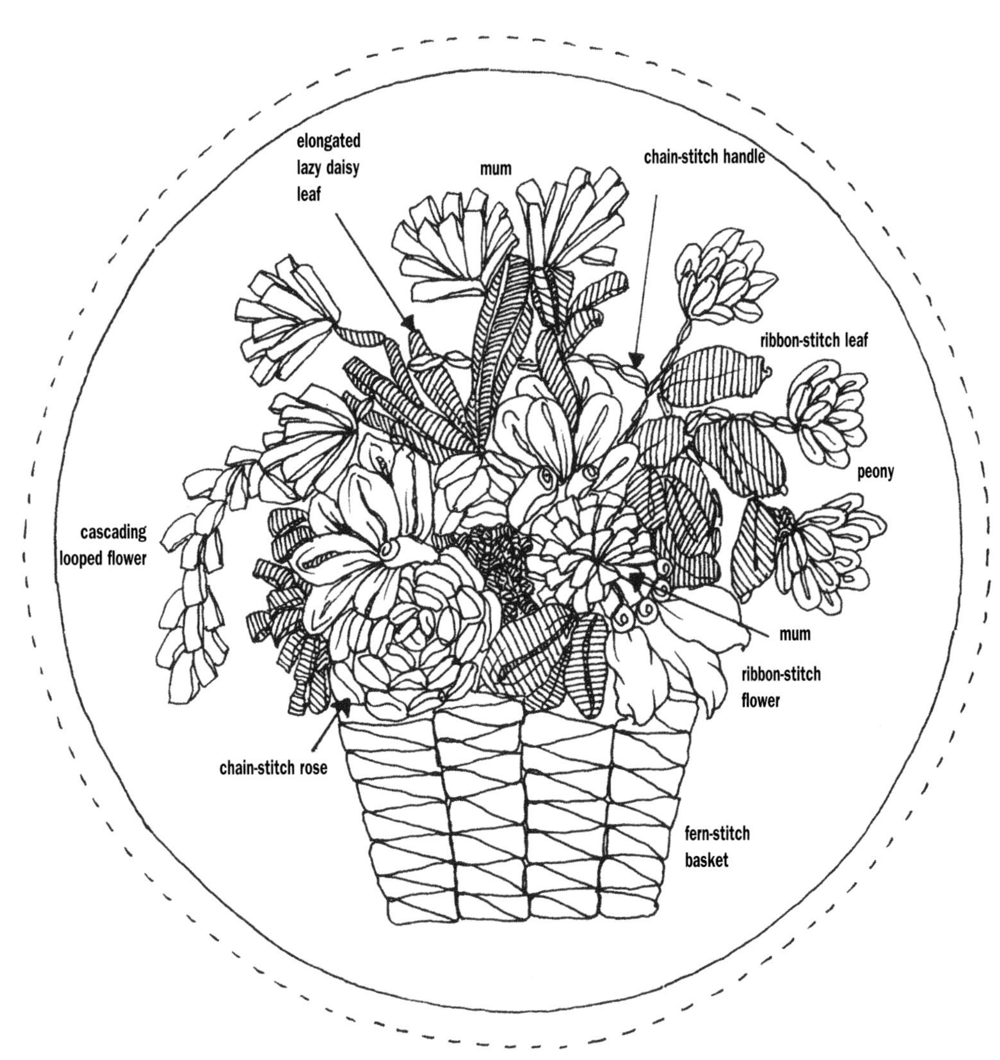

Floral Picture Mat

A frame bedecked with spring flowers makes a delightful vehicle for showing off your favorite embroidery as well as a keepsake photograph. Create this beautiful fabric mat and then use it in a purchased frame.

Materials

9" x 12" purchased oval-opening picture mat
½ yard of off-white linen or Aida cloth for mat
Ribbons: 2mm dark green and grayed green; 4mm light green, peach, grayed peach, grayed lavender, ecru, light blue, and light pink; 7mm white; light blue decorative thread
9" x 12" piece of polyester batting
12" x 18" piece of muslin for backing
9" x 12" purchased picture frame
Fabric glue
Hand sewing needles
Air-soluble marker

DIRECTIONS

1 Draw the outline of the mat and the inside opening on the linen and muslin pieces. Set the muslin piece aside. Draw flowers on the linen border as shown with an air-soluble marker.

2 Work flowers as shown.

3 Draw a cutting line on both the embellished and plain fabric pieces with an air-soluble marker 1½" around the outside line of the mat and ¾" inside the mat opening. Trim on the lines. Snip ⅝" into the fabric allowance around the mat opening.

4 Draw the outline of the mat and opening on polyester batting. Cut on the drawn lines. Glue the batting to the front of the mat.

5 Place the embellished fabric right side down on a clean work surface. Place the padded mat, batting side down, on top of the embellished fabric. Fold the edges of the embellished fabric to the back side of the mat around the outer and inner openings, and glue it in place.

6 Turn under the seam allowances on the muslin piece. Place the fabric on the back side of the mat and hand-stitch the fabrics together around all sides.

7 Insert mat in purchased frame.

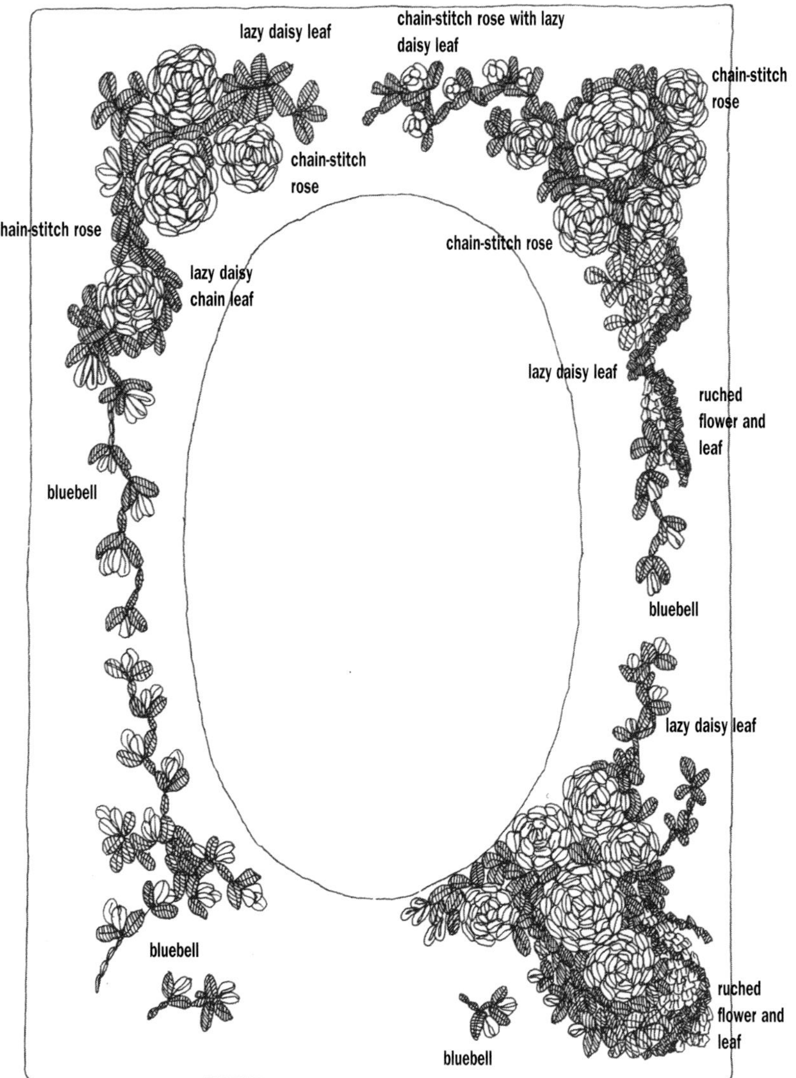

Floral Cascade on Jacket

Add a decidedly feminine touch to a purchased jacket. A bountiful cascade of embroidered spring flowers spilling over the shoulder makes this design a one-of-a-kind original.

Materials

Purchased jacket
Ribbons: 4mm light pink, medium pink, light rose, medium rose, magenta, purple, medium peach, bright yellow, light aqua, medium aqua, dark aqua, forest green, light avocado green, and light green
Air-soluble marker

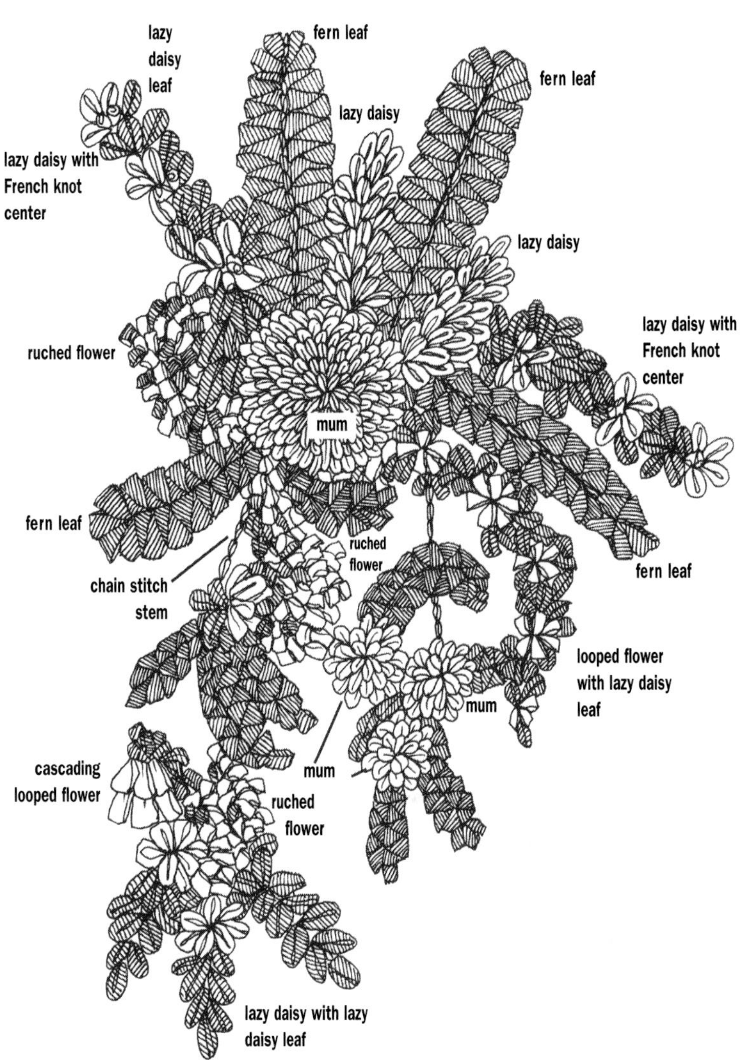

DIRECTIONS

1. Draw flowers on the jacket at the desired position with an air-soluble marker.
2. Work the flowers as shown.

Tips for Working on Purchased Garments

- Plan the location of your embroidery. The best places are the neckline; over a shoulder; down the center front of a blouse or jacket; on collars, cuffs, or yokes; down a skirt side front; and around a hem line. Remember—vertical or diagonal lines are slimming and horizontal lines aren't.
- Try on the garment to double-check the embroidery placement. Mark the area with an air-soluble marker.
- Remove the stitches that hold the lining in place in any areas of the garment that you'll embroider, and stitch only through a single layer of fabric. Restitch the lining when the embroidery is complete.
- For small pieces that won't easily fit into a hoop—such as collars and cuffs—baste the piece to a larger piece of scrap fabric. Cut away the scrap fabric in the area that you'll stitch, then fit your hoop over the entire fabric assembly. Work the embroidery and then remove the basting.

Crazy-Quilt Book Cover

An address book or journal is perfect for displaying a small sampler of crazy quilting. If you're making a vest, save the cut-away pieces for projects like this.

Materials

5" x 6" purchased address book or journal
Assorted scraps of velvet and satin fabrics
7" x 12½" piece of foundation fabric
Two 5¾" x 7" pieces of lining fabric
36" of satin piping
Ribbons: 4mm light green, medium green, fuchsia, light purple, plum, periwinkle, aqua, teal, light rose, and rose; 7mm lavender, dark green, and rose

DIRECTIONS

1. Work crazy quilting and stitches on foundation fabric as shown.

2. Pin and baste piping around the right side of embellished fabric piece ¼" from outer edge.

3. Turn one long edge of each lining piece under twice and stitch.

4. Pin and baste the right sides of flap lining pieces to the right side of embellished front. Stitch around outer edges with ¼" seam allowance. Clip corners and turn to right side. Press. Ease book into cover. (*Note: There is a 2" space at center to accommodate book binding.*)

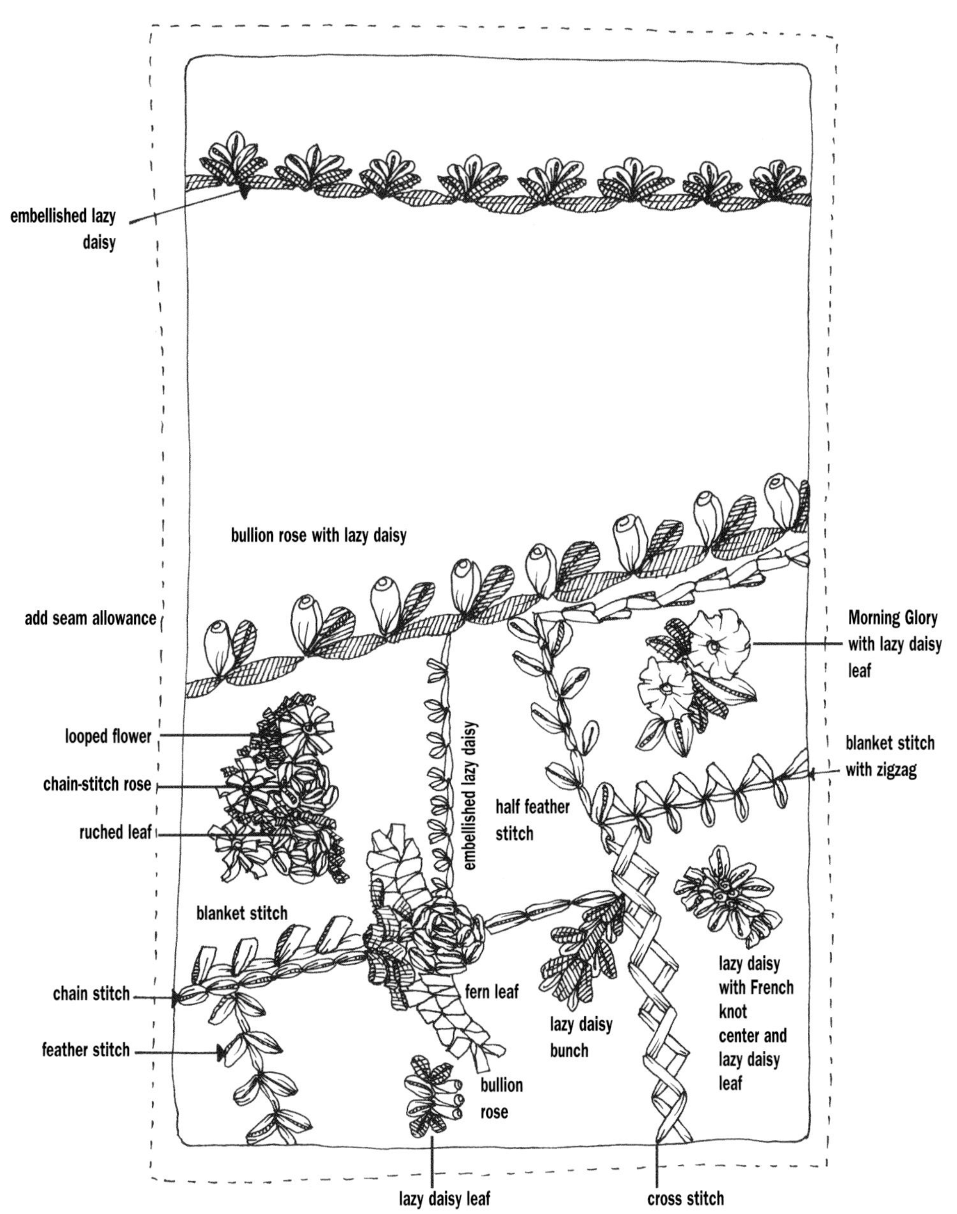

Crazy-Quilt Vest

Save bits and pieces of fabulous fabrics and use them to make a show-stopping crazy-quilt vest. Choose ribbon colors to contrast with the fabrics.

Materials

Commercial vest pattern
Assorted scraps of velvet and satin fabrics
1 yard of 44"-wide foundation fabric for working crazy-quilt vest fronts
Fabric for vest back (see the commercial pattern for requirements)
Fabric for lining (see the commercial pattern for requirements)
Ribbons: 4mm navy, light gray blue, gray blue, medium blue, teal, aqua, periwinkle, medium purple, cranberry, light garnet, garnet, turquoise, grayed peach, avocado green, medium green, and grayed green; 7mm grayed green and rose
Air-soluble marker or tailor's chalk
Permanent marker

DIRECTIONS

1. Cut the foundation fabric into two 18" x 22" pieces. Using the commercial pattern and a permanent marker, draw the shape of the vest front onto both foundation-fabric pieces, reversing one of them, so you have a left and right front.

2. Work crazy quilting and stitches as shown on both front foundation pieces using the marker lines as a guide. (Refer to crazy quilting instructions on pages 45–52.)

3. Pin the pattern pieces in place on embellished fabric and cut out the vest fronts, making sure you have a left and right.

4. Assemble the vest according to the pattern directions.

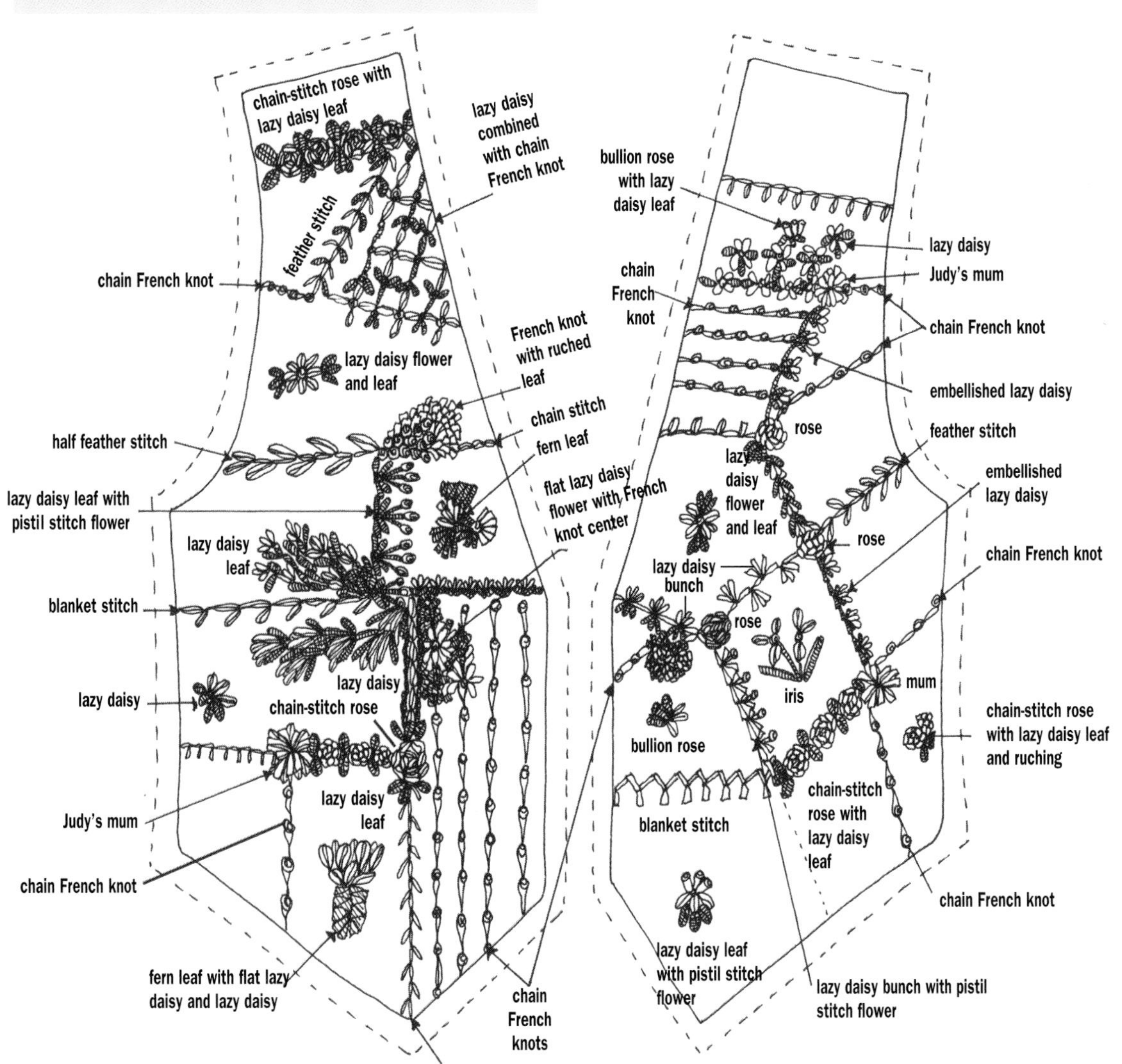

About the Authors

MARIE DUNCAN

I have been sewing for as long as I can remember. My mother sewed, and I remember matching navy-blue dresses she made us with big white buttons down the front. I started sewing doll clothes, and took home economics in 7th and 8th grades. Other than one tailoring class in high school, that is the extent of my formal education in sewing.

Sewing has always been enjoyable. In the summer, in high school, I would get on my bike and go to the local department store with $5 and come home with fabric for an outfit, which would keep me busy for days.

My formal education is an associate degree in commercial art. Although I worked in the field for only a year, I have used that art background in almost everything I have done in life, from raising my daughter to my real career, teaching sewing and selling sewing and knitting machines.

When my daughter was in kindergarten, I answered a help-wanted ad for someone with sewing experience. That led to a job selling sewing machines in a local fabric store. I've been in this field ever since. I've had my own sewing-machine dealership, worked for other dealers, and traveled nationally for a major sewing-machine company. Throughout my various travels and jobs, I have continued to learn about and enjoy sewing. I've been at Andrews Company for nine years, selling sewing machines and teaching all kinds of classes. Even now, after working with sewing machines all day, I still find it relaxing to go home and sew.

It's been a new experience writing a book. Although I can't be there to hold your hand and tell you what to do, it's a real joy to know that I'm able to share the joy of ribbon embroidery with so many of you. I hope you enjoy our book as much as we've enjoyed writing it.

BETTY FARRELL

My sewing began as a freshman in high school, where home economics was a required part of the curriculum for girls. I found I enjoyed sewing and creating clothes. It was difficult to "just follow the pattern" and not add my own personal touches. But it was a great way to add to my wardrobe when funds were limited.

When college beckoned, I pursued a major in home economics at Iowa State University in Ames, Iowa. After graduation, I taught kindergarten, preferring that age level to older students. Then, sewing was a necessity as well as a creative outlet. And ever since, I've always had several projects in varying degrees of completion—gifts, things for the children or the house, or something for myself.

Besides teaching, my professional career has included marketing, public relations, sales, and being a district manager for a major sewing-machine company. Right now, I'm doing sales, marketing, seminars, and purchasing for Brewer Sewing Supplies (a wholesale sewing-supply distributor). In this position, I am exposed to all of the books, threads, ribbons, and notions that emerge for the creative sewer and crafter to enjoy.

I hope you too will find ribbon embroidery by machine to be a wonderful outlet for your creative energies. I have done ribbon embroidery both by hand and machine, and I find them both beautiful and addictive. Ribbon embroidery by machine is so versatile! Take our ideas, adapt them to your own needs, and enjoy the wonderful things you create for yourself, your home, and your friends.

Sources

Check at your local fabric, crafts, or yarn store for a stock of ribbons. If you can't find what you're looking for, here are some national mail-order suppliers:

ANDREWS COMPANY
Attn: Marie Duncan
1016 Davis
Evanston, IL 60201
1-800-870-0404

CLOTILDE
2 Smart Way
B 8031
Stevens Point, WI 54481
1-800-772-2891

NANCY'S NOTIONS
333 Beichl Avenue
P.O. Box 683
Beaver Dam, WI 53916
414-887-0391

QUILTERS' RESOURCE INC.
P.O. Box 148850
Chicago, IL 60614
1-800-676-6543

YLI CORPORATION
P.O. Box 109
Provo, UT 84603
801-377-3900

Index